The Heel of Achilles ESSAYS 1968–1973

Books by Arthur Koestler

Novels
THE GLADIATORS*
DARKNESS AT NOON*
ARRIVAL AND DEPARTURE*
THIEVES IN THE NIGHT*
THE AGE OF LONGING*
THE CALL-GIRLS

Autobiography
DIALOGUE WITH DEATH*
SCUM OF THE EARTH*
ARROW IN THE BLUE*
THE INVISIBLE WRITING*
THE GOD THAT FAILED (with others)

Essays
THE YOGI AND THE COMMISSAR*
INSIGHT AND OUTLOOK
PROMISE AND FULFILMENT
THE TRAIL OF THE DINOSAUR*
REFLECTIONS ON HANGING*
THE SLEEPWALKERS*
THE LOTUS AND THE ROBOT*
THE ACT OF CREATION*
THE GHOST IN THE MACHINE
DRINKERS OF INFINITY
THE CASE OF THE MIDWIFE TOAD
THE ROOTS OF COINCIDENCE
THE CHALLENGE OF CHANCE
(with Sir Alister Hardy and Robert Harvie)
SUICIDE OF A NATION (ed.)
BEYOND REDUCTIONISM: THE ALPBACH SYMPOSIUM
(ed. with J. R. Smythies)

Theatre
TWILIGHT BAR

*Available in the Danube Edition

The Heel of Achilles
Essays 1968–1973
Arthur Koestler

HUTCHINSON OF LONDON

Hutchinson & Co (Publishers) Ltd
3 Fitzroy Square, London W1

London Melbourne Sydney Auckland
Wellington Johannesburg Cape Town
and agencies throughout the world

First published 1974
© Arthur Koestler 1968, 1969, 1970, 1971, 1972, 1973

Set in Monotype Baskerville
Printed in Great Britain by
Ebenezer Baylis & Son Limited
The Trinity Press, Worcester, and London
and bound by Wm Brendon, Tiptree, Essex

ISBN 0 09 119400 8

Contents

Contents

'Nothing But . . .'?

Excursions and Pilgrimages

Mahatma Gandhi – Yogi and Commissar

Preface

As in the case of the last collection of essays (*Drinkers of Infinity*, 1968), the present volume again consists of writings and lectures addressed to such varied audiences as the Nobel Foundation, the World Psychiatric Association, universities and scientific conferences – but also to the broader readership of *The Times*, the *Sunday Times*, the *Observer*, etc. The items in the collection thus differ in style and weight, ranging from excursions into journalism to academic papers which are somewhat technical – but not too technical, I hope, for the general reader. Yet in spite of their diversity, these essays were intended as variations on certain themes, and are grouped accordingly. The first section has as its leitmotiv the predicament of man; the book reviews, too, have a certain thematic coherence and are related to that theme; the section called 'Nothing But . . .'? attacks the prevailing materialistic philosophy from different angles; and even the article on chess champions and chess computers has a direct bearing on the subject of Mind and Machine.

The last essay, dealing with certain disastrous aspects of Gandhi's life and philosophy – which are largely unknown to the public – is intended to redress the balance by stressing the dangers of taking shortcuts from Western materialism to Eastern mysticism.

A.K.

The Heel of Achilles

The Urge to Self-destruction*

The crisis of our time can be summed up in a single sentence. From the dawn of consciousness until the middle of our century man had to live with the prospect of his death as an individual; since Hiroshima, mankind as a whole has to live with the prospect of its extinction as a biological species.

This is a radically new prospect; but though the novelty of it will wear off, the prospect will not; it has become a basic and permanent feature of the human condition.

There are periods of incubation before a new idea takes hold of the mind; the Copernican doctrine which so radically downgraded man's status in the universe took nearly a century until it got a hold on European consciousness. The new downgrading of our species to the status of mortality is even more difficult to digest.

But there are signs that in a devious, roundabout way the process of mental assimilation has already started. It is as if the explosions had produced a kind of psychoactive fall-out, particularly in the younger generation, creating such bizarre phenomena as hippies, drop-outs, flower people and barefoot crusaders without a cross. They seem to be products of a kind of mental radiation sickness which causes an intense and distressing experience of meaninglessness, of an existential

* Edited version of the Sonning Prize Acceptance Address to the University of Copenhagen, April 1968, and of a paper read at the Fourteenth Nobel Symposium, Stockholm, September 1969.

vacuum which the traditional values of their elders are unable to fill.

These symptoms will probably wear off. Already the word Hiroshima has become a historic cliché like the Boston Tea Party or the Storming of the Bastille. Sooner or later we shall return to a state of pseudo-normality. But there is no getting away from the fact that from now onward our species lives on borrowed time. It carries a time-bomb fastened round its neck. We shall have to listen to the sound of its ticking, now louder, now softer, now louder again, for decades and centuries to come, until it either blows up, or we succeed in de-fusing it.

Our concern is with the possibility of such a de-fusing operation. Obviously it requires more than disarmament conferences and appeals to sweet reasonableness. They have always fallen on deaf ears, for the simple reason that man is perhaps a sweet, but certainly not a reasonable being; nor are there any indications that he is in the process of becoming one. On the contrary, the evidence seems to indicate that at some point during the last explosive stages of the biological evolution of *homo sapiens* something has gone wrong; that there is a flaw, some subtle engineering mistake built into our native equipment which would account for the paranoid streak running through our history. This seems to me an unpleasant but plausible hypothesis, which I have developed at some length in a recent book.[1] Evolution has made countless mistakes; Sir Julian Huxley compared it to a maze with an enormous number of blind alleys. For every existing species hundreds must have perished in the past; the fossil record is a wastebasket of the Chief Designer's discarded hypotheses. To the biologist, it should appear by no means unlikely that *homo sapiens*, too, is the victim of some minute error in construction – perhaps in the circuitry of his nervous system – which makes him prone to delusions, and urges him towards self-destruction. But *homo sapiens* has also the unique resourcefulness to transcend biological evolution and to compensate for the shortcomings of his native equipment. He may even have the power to cure that congenitally dis-ordered mental condition which played havoc with his past and now threatens him with extinction. Or, if he cannot cure it, at least to render it harmless.

The first step towards a possible therapy is a correct diagnosis. There have been countless diagnostic attempts, from the Hebrew prophets to contemporary ethologists, but none of them sounded very convincing, because none of them started from the premiss that man is an aberrant species, suffering from a biological malfunction, a species-specific disorder of behaviour which sets it apart from all other animal species – just as language, science and art sets it apart in a positive sense. The creativity and the pathology of man are two sides of the same medal, coined in the same evolutionary mint. I am going to propose a short list of some of the pathological symptoms reflected in the perverse history of our species, and then pass from the symptoms to the presumed causative factors. The list of symptoms has five main headings.

First, at the very beginning of history, we find a striking phenomenon to which anthropologists seem to have paid too little attention: human sacrifice. It was a ubiquitous ritual which persisted from the prehistoric dawn to the peak of pre-Columbian civilizations, and in some parts of the world to the beginning of our century. From the Scandinavian Bog People to the South Sea Islanders, from the Etruscans to the pre-Columbian cultures, these practices arose independently in the most varied civilizations, as manifestations of a perverted logic to which the whole species was apparently prone. It is epitomized in one of the early chapters of Genesis, where Abraham prepares to cut the throat of his son out of sheer love of God. Instead of dismissing the subject as a sinister curiosity of the past, the universality and para-noid character of the ritual should be regarded as symptomatic.

The *second* symptom to be noted is the weakness of the inhibitory forces against the killing of con-specifics, which is virtually unique in the animal kingdom. As Konrad Lorenz[2] has recently emphasized, the predator's act of killing the prey should not be compared to murder, and not even be called aggressive, because predator and prey always belong to different species – a hawk killing a fieldmouse can hardly be accused of homicide. Competition and conflict between members of the same animal species is settled by ritualized combat or symbolic threat-behaviour which ends with the flight or surrender gesture of one of the combatants, and hardly ever involves lethal injury. In man, however, this built-in inhibitory mechanism against killing con-specifics is notably ineffective.

This leads to the *third* symptom: intraspecific warfare in permanence, with its sub-varieties of mass persecution and genocide. The popular confusion between predatory and bellicose behaviour tends to obscure the fact that the law of the jungle permits predation on other species, but forbids war within one's own; and that *homo sapiens* is the unique offender against this law (apart from some controversial warlike phenomena among rats and ants).

As the *fourth* symptom I would list the permanent, quasi-schizophrenic split between reason and emotion, between man's critical faculties and his irrational, affect-charged beliefs; I shall return to this point.

Lastly, there is the striking, symptomatic disparity between the growth-curves of technological achievement on the one hand and of ethical behaviour on the other; or, to put it differently, between the powers of the intellect when applied to mastering the environment, and its impotence when applied to the conduct of human affairs. In the sixth century B.C. the Greeks embarked on the scientific adventure which, a few months ago, landed us on the moon. That surely is an impressive growth-curve. But the sixth century B.C. also saw the birth of Taoism, Confucianism and Buddhism; the twentieth of Stalinism, Hitlerism and Maoism. There is no discernible curve. We can control the motions of satellites orbiting the distant planets but cannot control the situation

in Northern Ireland. Prometheus is reaching out for the
stars with an empty grin on his face and a totem-symbol in
his hand.

So far we have moved in the realm of facts. When we turn
from *symptoms* to *causes*, we must have recourse to more or
less speculative hypotheses. I shall mention five such hypotheses, which are interrelated, but pertain to different
disciplines, namely neurophysiology, anthropology, psychology, linguistics, and lastly eschatology.

The neurophysiological hypothesis is derived from the
so-called Papez–MacLean theory of emotions. Though still
controversial in some respects, it is supported by twenty
years of experimental research, and has for quite some years
attained textbook respectability. The theory is based on the
structural and functional differences between the phylogenetically old and recent parts in the human brain which,
when not in acute conflict, seem to lead a kind of agonized
coexistence. Dr MacLean has summed up this state of affairs
in a technical paper, but in an unusually picturesque way:

> Man finds himself in the predicament that nature has endowed
> him essentially with three brains which, despite great differences
> in structure, must function together and communicate with one
> another. The oldest of these brains is basically reptilian. The
> second has been inherited from lower mammals, and the third is a
> late mammalian development, which . . . has made man peculiarly
> man. Speaking allegorically of these brains within a brain, we
> might imagine that when the psychiatrist bids the patient to lie
> on the couch, he is asking him to stretch out alongside a horse and
> a crocodile.[3]

Substitute for the individual patient humanity at large, for
the clinical couch the stage of history, and you get a dramatized, but essentially truthful, picture. The reptilian and
primitive mammalian brain together form the so-called
limbic system which, for simplicity's sake, we may call the
old brain, as opposed to the neocortex, the specifically human
'thinking-cap' which contains the areas responsible for
language, and abstract and symbolic thought. The neocortex

of the hominids evolved in the last half-million years, from the middle Pleistocene onward, at an explosive speed, which as far as we know is unprecedented in the history of evolution. This brain explosion in the second half of the Pleistocene seems to have followed the type of exponential curve which has recently become so familiar to us – population explosion, knowledge explosion, etc. – and there may be more than a superficial analogy here, as both curves reflect the phenomenon of the acceleration of history on different levels. But explosions do not produce harmonious results. The result in this particular case seems to have been that the newly developing structures did not become properly integrated with the phylogenetically older ones – an evolutionary blunder which provided rich opportunities for conflict. MacLean coined the term *schizophysiology* for this precarious state of affairs in our nervous system. He defines it as

a dichotomy in the function of the phylogenetically old and new cortex that might account for differences between emotional and intellectual behaviour. While our intellectual functions are carried on in the newest and most highly developed part of the brain, our affective behaviour continues to be dominated by a relatively crude and primitive system, by archaic structures in the brain whose fundamental pattern has undergone but little change in the whole course of evolution, from mouse to man.[4]

To put it crudely: evolution has left a few screws loose somewhere between the neocortex and the hypothalamus. The hypothesis that this form of schizophysiology is built into our species could go a long way to explain symptoms Nos. 4 and 5. The delusional streak in our history, the prevalence of passionately held irrational beliefs, would at last become comprehensible and could be expressed in physiological terms. And any condition which can be expressed in physiological terms should ultimately be accessible to remedies.

My next two putative causes of man's predicament are the state of protracted dependence of the neonate on its parents, and the dependence of the earliest carnivorous hominids on the support of their hunting companions against prey faster and more powerful than themselves; a mutual dependence much stronger than that among other primate groups, out of which may have developed tribal solidarity and its later nefarious derivatives. Both factors may have contributed to the process of moulding man into the loyal, affectionate and sociable creature which he is; the trouble is that they did it only too well and overshot the mark. The bonds forged by early helplessness and mutual dependence developed into various forms of bondsmanship within the family, clan or tribe. The helplessness of the human infant leaves its lifelong mark; it may be partly responsible for man's ready submission to authority wielded by individuals or groups, his quasi-hypnotic suggestibility by doctrines and commandments, his overwhelming urge to belong, to identify himself with tribe or nation, and, above all, with its system of beliefs. Brain-washing starts in the cradle. (Konrad Lorenz uses the analogy of imprinting, and puts the critical age of receptivity just after puberty. But there are two limitations to this analogy: the susceptibility for imprinting stretches in man from the cradle to the grave; and what he is imprinted with are mostly symbols.)

Now, historically speaking, for the vast majority of mankind, the belief-system which they accepted, for which they were prepared to live or die, was not of their own choice, but imposed on them by the hazards of the social environment, just as their tribal or ethnic identity was determined by the hazards of birth. Critical reasoning played, if any, only a subordinate part in the process of accepting the imprint of a credo. If the tenets of the credo were too offensive to the critical faculties, schizophysiology provided the *modus vivendi* which permitted the hostile forces of faith and reason to coexist in a universe of doublethink – to use Orwell's term.

Thus one of the central features of the human predicament is this overwhelming capacity and need for identification with a social group and/or a system of beliefs which is indifferent to reason, indifferent to self-interest and even to the

B   17 claims of self-preservation. Extreme manifestations of this *self-transcending tendency* – as one might call it – are the hypnotic rapport, a variety of trance-like or ecstatic states, the phenomena of individual and collective suggestibility which dominate life in primitive and not so primitive societies, culminating in mass hysteria in its overt and latent form. One need not march in a crowd to become a victim of crowd-mentality – the true believer is its captive all the time.

We are thus driven to the unfashionable and uncomfortable conclusion that the trouble with our species is not an over-dose of self-asserting *aggression*, but an excess of self-transcending *devotion*. Even a cursory glance at history should convince one that individual crimes committed for selfish motives play a quite insignificant role in the human tragedy compared with the numbers massacred in unselfish love of one's tribe, nation, dynasty, church or ideology. The emphasis is on unselfish. Excepting a small minority of mercenary or sadistic disposition, wars are not fought for personal gain, but out of loyalty and devotion to king, country or cause.

Homicide committed for personal reasons is a statistical rarity in all cultures, including our own. Homicide for *un*-selfish reasons, at the risk of one's own life, is the dominant phenomenon in history. Even the members of the Mafia feel compelled to rationalize their motives into an ideology, the Cosa Nostra, 'our cause'.

The theory that wars are caused by pent-up aggressive drives which can find no other outlet has no foundation either in history or in psychology. Anybody who has served in the ranks of an army can testify that aggressive feelings towards the so-called enemy hardly play a part in the dreary routine of waging war: boredom and discomfort, not hatred; homesickness, sex-starvation and longing for peace dominate the mind of the anonymous soldier. The invisible enemy is not an individual on whom aggression could focus; he is not a person but an abstract entity, a common denominator, a collective portrait. Soldiers fight the invisible, impersonal enemy either because they have no other choice, or out of loyalty to king and country, the true religion, the righteous cause. They are motivated not by aggression, but by *devotion*.

I am equally unconvinced by the fashionable theory that the philogenetic origin of war is to be found in the so-called 'territorial imperative'. The wars of man, with rare exceptions, were not fought for individual ownership of bits of space. The man who goes to war actually *leaves* the home which he is supposed to defend, and engages in combat hundreds or thousands of miles away from it; and what makes him fight is not the biological urge to defend his personal acreage of farmland or meadows, but – to say it once more – his loyalty to symbols and slogans derived from tribal lore, divine commandments or political ideologies. Wars are fought for words. They are motivated not by aggression, but by love.

We have seen on the screen the radiant love of the Führer on the faces of the Hitler Youth. We have seen the same expression on the faces of little Chinese boys reciting the words of the Chairman. They are transfixed with love like monks in ecstasy on religious paintings. The sound of the nation's anthem, the sight of its proud flag, makes you feel part of a wonderfully loving community.

Thus, in opposition to Lorenz, Ardrey and their followers, I would suggest that the trouble with our species is not an excess of aggression, but an excess of devotion. The fanatic is prepared to lay down his life for the object of his worship as the lover is prepared to die for his idol. He is equally prepared to kill anybody who represents a supposed threat to that idol. Here we come to a point of central importance. You watch a film version of the Moor of Venice. You fall in love with Desdemona and identify yourself with Othello (or the other way round); as a result the perfidious Iago makes your blood boil. Yet the psychological process which causes the boiling is quite different from facing a real opponent. You know that the people on the screen are merely actors or rather electronic projections – and anyway the whole situation is no personal concern of yours. The adrenalin in your bloodstream is not produced by a primary biological drive or hypothetical killer-instinct. Your hostility to Iago is a *vicarious* kind of aggressivity, devoid of self-interest and derived from a previous process of empathy and identification. This act of identification must come first; it is the *conditio sine qua non*, the trigger or catalyst of your dislike of Iago. In the same way, the savagery unleashed in primitive forms of warfare is also triggered by a previous act of identification with a social group, its rousing symbols and system of beliefs. It is a depersonalized, quite unselfish kind of savagery, generated by the group-mind, *which is largely indifferent, or even opposed, to the interests of the individuals who constitute the group*. Identification with the group always involves a sacrifice of the individual's critical faculties, and an enhancement of his emotional potential by a kind of group-resonance or positive feedback. Thus the mentality of the group is not the sum of individual minds; it has its own pattern and obeys its own rules which cannot be 'reduced' to the rules which govern individual behaviour. The individual is not a killer; the group is, and by identifying with it the individual is transformed into a killer. This is the infernal dialectics reflected in our history. The egotism of the group feeds on the altruism of its members; the savagery of the group feeds on the devotion of its members.

All this points to the conclusion that the predicament of man is not caused by the aggressivity of the individual, but by the dialectics of group-formation; by man's irresistible urge to identify with the group and espouse its beliefs enthusiastically and uncritically. He has a peculiar capacity – and need – to become emotionally committed to beliefs which are impervious to reasoning, indifferent to self-interest and even to the claims of self-preservation. Waddington has called man a belief-accepting animal. He is as susceptible to being imprinted with slogans and symbols as he is to infectious diseases. Thus one of the main pathogenic factors is hyper-dependence combined with suggestibility. If science could find a way to make us immune against suggestibility, half the battle for survival would be won. And this does not seem to be an impossible target.

The next item in this inventory of the possible causes of man's predicament is language. Let me repeat: wars are fought for words. They are man's most deadly weapon. The words of Adolf Hitler were more effective agents of destruction than thermonuclear bombs. Long before the printing press and the other mass media were invented, the fervent words of the prophet Mohammed released an emotive chain-reaction, whose blast shook the world from Central Asia to the Atlantic coast. Without words there would be no poetry – and no war. Language is the main source of our superiority over brother animal – and, in view of its explosive potentials, the main threat to our survival.

Recent field-studies of Japanese monkeys have revealed that different tribes of a species may develop surprisingly different habits – one might almost say, different cultures. Some tribes have taken to washing bananas in the river before eating them, others do not. Sometimes migrating groups of banana-washers meet non-washers, and the two groups watch each other's strange behaviour with apparent bewilderment. But unlike the inhabitants of Lilliput, who fought holy crusades over the question whether eggs should be broken on the broad or pointed end, the banana-washing monkeys do not go to war with the non-washers, because the poor creatures have no language which would enable them to declare washing an ethical commandment and eating unwashed bananas a deadly heresy.

Obviously, the safest remedy for our ills would be to abolish language. But as a matter of fact, mankind did renounce language long ago – if by language we mean a universal means of communication for the whole species. Other species do possess a single system of communication by sign, sound or odour, which is understood by all its members. Dolphins travel a lot, and when two strangers meet in the ocean they need no interpreter. The Tower of Babel has remained a valid symbol. According to Margaret Mead, among the two million Aborigines in New Guinea, 750 different languages are spoken in 750 villages, which are at permanent war with one another. Our shrinking planet is split into several thousand language-groups. Each language acts as a powerful cohesive force within the group and as an equally powerful divisive force between groups. Fleming detests Walloon, Maharati hates Gujerati, French Canadian despises Anglo-Saxon, differences in accent mark the boundary between the upper and lower classes within the same nation.

Thus language appears to be one of the main reasons, perhaps *the* main reason, why the disruptive forces have always been stronger than the cohesive forces in our species. One might even ask whether the term 'species' is applicable to man. I have mentioned that Lorenz attributed great importance to the instinct-taboo among animals against the killing of members of their own species; yet it may be argued that Greeks killing Barbarians, Moors killing Christian dogs did not perceive their victims as members of their own species. Aristotle expressly stated that 'the slave is totally devoid of any faculty of reasoning'; the term Bar-bar-ous is imitative of the alien's gibberish or the barking of a dog; honest Nazis believed that Jews were *Untermenschen* – not human but hominid. Men show a much greater variety in physique and behaviour than any animal species (except for the domesticated products of selective breeding); and language, instead of counteracting intraspecific tensions and fratricidal tendencies, enhances their virulence. It is a grotesque paradox that we have communication satellites which can make a message visible and audible over the whole planet, but no planet-wide language to make it also understandable. It seems even more odd that, except for a few stalwart Esperantists, neither Unesco nor any other international body has made a serious effort to promote a universal *lingua franca* – as the dolphins have.

The fifth and last pathogenic factor on my list is man's awareness of his mortality, the discovery of death. But one should rather say: its discovery by the intellect, and its rejection by instinct and emotion. We may assume that the inevitability of death was discovered, through inductive inference, by that newly acquired thinking-cap, the human neocortex; but the old brain won't have any of it; emotion rebels against the idea of personal non-existence. This simultaneous acceptance and refusal of death reflects perhaps the deepest split in man's split mind; it saturated the air with ghosts and demons, invisible presences which at best were inscrutable, but mostly malevolent, and had to be appeased by human sacrifice, by holy wars and the burning of heretics. The paranoid delusions of eternal hell-fire are still with us. Paradise was always an exclusive club, but the gates of hell were open to all.

Yet once more we have to look at both sides of the medal: on one side religious art, architecture and music in the cathedral; on the other, the paranoid delusions of eternal hell-fire, the tortures of the living and the dead.

To sum up, I have listed five conspicuous symptoms of the pathology of man as reflected in the terrible mess we have made, and continue to make, of our history. I have mentioned the ubiquitous rites of sacrifice in the prehistoric dawn; the poverty of instinct-inhibition against the killing of conspecifics: intraspecific warfare in permanence; the schizoid split between rational thinking and irrational beliefs; and lastly the contrast between man's genius in mastering the environment and his moronic conduct of human affairs. It should be noted that each and all of these pathological phenomena are species-specific, that they are uniquely human, not found in any other animal species. It is only logical therefore that in the search for explanations we should concentrate our attention on those characteristics of man which are also exclusively human and not shared by other animals. Speaking in all humility, it seems to me of doubtful value to attempt a diagnosis of man entirely based on analogies with animal behaviour – Pavlov's dogs, Skinner's rats, Lorenz's greylag geese, Morris's hairless apes. Such analogies are valid and useful as far as they go. But by the nature of things they cannot go far enough, because they stop short of those exclusively human characteristics – such as language – which are of necessity excluded from the analogy, although they are of decisive importance in determining the behaviour of our species. There is no human arrogance involved in saying that dogs, rats, birds and apes do not have a neocortex which has evolved too fast for the good of its possessor; that they do not share the protracted helplessness of the human infant, nor the strong mutual dependence and *esprit de corps* of the ancestral hunters. Nor the dangerous privilege of using words to coin battle-cries; nor the inductive powers which make men frightened to death by death. These character-istics which I have mentioned as possible causative factors of the human predicament, are all specifically and exclusively human. They contribute to the uniqueness of man and the uniqueness of his tragedy. They combine in the double helix of guilt and anxiety which, like the genetic code, seems to be built into the human condition. They give indeed ample cause for anxiety regarding our future; but then, another unique gift of man is the power to make his anxiety work for him. He may even manage to de-fuse the time-bomb around his neck, once he has understood the mechanisms which make it tick. Biological evolution seems to have come to a standstill since the days of Cro-Magnon man; since we can-not expect in the foreseeable future a beneficial mutation to put things right, our only hope seems to be to supplant biological evolution by new, as yet undreamt-of techniques. In my more optimistic moments my split brain suggests that this possibility may not be beyond our reach.

REFERENCES

1. *The Ghost in the Machine* (London and New York, 1968).
2. K. Lorenz, *On Aggression* (London and New York, 1966).

3. *Journal of Nervous and Mental Diseases*, Vol. cxxxv, No. 4, October 1962.
4. *American Journal of Medicine*, Vol. xxv, No. 4, October 1958.

Rebellion in a Vacuum*

Hoping to discover at long last what the verb 'to educate' means, I turned the other day to the *Concise Oxford Dictionary* and was amused to find this definition : 'Give intellectual and moral training to.' And further down, to drive the nail home : 'Train (person) . . . train (animals).' I would not be surprised to see, when the next rioting season starts, a bonfire of *Oxford Dictionaries*; and that definition, with its Pavlovian echoes, certainly deserves no better. But I am doubtful whether much would be gained by replacing the offensive term 'training' by 'guidance'. That sounds nice and smarmy, but it begs the question. Guiding, by whatever discreet methods, always implies asserting one's mental powers over another person's mind – in the present context, a younger person's. And the ethics of this procedure, which not so long ago we took for granted, is becoming more and more problematical.

My own preference is for defining the purpose of education as 'catalysing the mind'. To influence is to intrude ; a catalyst, on the other hand, is defined as an agent that triggers or speeds up a chemical reaction without being involved in the

* Revised version of a paper prepared for the symposium 'The University and the Ethics of Change' at Queen's University, Kingston, Canada, November 1968. First published in *The Political Quarterly*, October–December 1969.

product. If I may utter a truism, the ideal educator acts as a catalyst, not as a conditioning influence. Conditioning or, to use Skinner's term, 'social engineering through the control of behaviour', is an excellent method for training samurais, but applied on the campus it has two opposite dangers. It may lead to a kind of experimental neurosis in the subjects, expressed by violent rejection of any control or influence by authority. On the other hand, it can be too successful, and create the phenomena of conformism, with a broad spectrum ranging from a society of placid yes-men manipulated by the mass media to the totalitarian state controlled by the Thoughts of Chairman Mao.

The alternative to conditioning is catalysing the mind's development. I can best explain what is meant by quoting a passage from a book I wrote some years ago on creativity in science and art.

To enable the student to derive pleasure from the art of scientific discovery, as from other forms of art, he should be made to re-live, to some extent, the creative process. In other words, he must be induced, with proper aid and guidance, to make some of the fundamental discoveries of science by himself, to experience in his own mind some of those flashes of insight which have lightened its path. This means that the history of science ought to be made an essential part of the curriculum, that science should be re-presented in its evolutionary context – not as a Minerva born fully armed. It further means that the paradoxes, the 'blocked problems' which confronted Archimedes, Copernicus, Galileo, Newton, Harvey, Darwin, should be reconstructed in their historical setting and presented in the form of riddles – with appropriate hints – to eager young minds. The most productive form of learning is problem-solving. The traditional method of confronting the student, not with the problem but with the finished solution, means to deprive him of all excitement, to shut off the creative impulse, to reduce the adventure of mankind to a dusty heap of theorems.

Art is a form of communication which aims at eliciting a re-creative echo. Education should be regarded as an art, and use the appropriate techniques to call forth that echo – the 'recreation'. The novice, who has gone through some of the main stages in the evolution of the species during his embryonic development, and through the evolution from savage to civilized society by the time he reaches adolescence, should then be made to continue his curriculum by recapitulating some of the decisive episodes, impasses, and turning-points on the road to the conquest of knowledge. Much in our textbooks and methods of teaching reflects a static, pre-evolutionary concept of the world. For man cannot inherit the past; he has to re-create it.[1]

This is what I meant by education as a catalytic process. But now comes the rub. Assuming we agree that the ideal method of teaching science is to enable the student to re-discover Newton's Laws of Motion more or less by himself – can the same method be applied to the teaching of ethics, of moral values? The first answer that comes to mind is that ethics is not a discipline in the normal curriculum, except if you specialize in philosophy or theology. But that is a rash answer, because implicitly, if not explicitly, we impart ethical principles and value-judgements in whatever we teach or write on whatever subject. The greatest superstition of our time is the belief in the ethical neutrality of science. Even the slogan of ethical neutrality itself implies a programme and a credo.

No writer or teacher or artist can escape the responsibility of influencing others, whether he intends to or not, whether he is conscious of it or not. And this influence is not confined to his explicit message; it is the more powerful and the more insidious because much of it is transmitted implicitly, as a hidden persuader, and the recipient absorbs it unawares. Surely physics is an ethically neutral science? Yet Einstein rejected the trend in modern physics to replace causality by probability with his famous dictum: 'I refuse to believe that God plays dice with the world.' He was more honest than other physicists in admitting his metaphysical bias; and it is precisely this metaphysical bias, implied in a scientific hypothesis, which exerts its unconscious influence on others. The Roman Church was ill advised when she opposed Galileo and Darwin, and from a rational point of view was lagging behind the times; but intuitively she was ahead of the times in realizing the impact which the new cosmology and the theory of evolution was to have on man's image of himself and his place in the universe.

Wolfgang Köhler, one of the greatest psychologists of our time, searched all his life for 'the place of value in a world of facts' – the title of the book in which he summed up his personal philosophy. But there is no need to search for such a place because the values are diffused through all the strata of the various sciences, as the invisible bubbles of air are diffused in the waters of a lake, and we are the fish who breathe them in all the time through the gills of intuition. Our educational establishment, from the departments of physics through biology and genetics, up to the behavioural and social sciences, willy-nilly imparts to the students a *Weltanschauung*, a system of values wrapped up in a package of facts. But the choice and shape of the package is determined by its invisible content; or, to change the metaphor, our implicit values provide the non-Euclidian curvature, the subtle distortions of the world of facts.

Now when I use the term 'our educational establishment', you may object that there is no such thing. Every country, every university and every faculty therein has of course its individual character, its personal face – or facelessness. Nevertheless, taking diversity for granted, and exceptions for granted, there exist certain common denominators which determine the cultural climate and the metaphysical bias imparted to hopeful students practically everywhere in the non-totalitarian sector of the world, from California to the East Coast, from London to Berlin, Bombay and Tokyo. That climate is impossible to define without oversimplification, so I shall oversimplify deliberately and say that it is dominated by three Rs.

The first R stands for Reductionism. Its philosophy may be epitomized by a quotation from a recent book in which man is defined, in all seriousness, as 'nothing but a complex biochemical mechanism, powered by a combustion system which energizes computers with prodigious storage facilities for retaining encoded information'. This is certainly an extreme formulation, but it conveys the essence of that philosophy.

It is, of course, perfectly legitimate to draw analogies between the central nervous system and a telephone exchange, or a computer, or a holograph. The reductionist heresy is contained in the words 'nothing but'. If you replace in the sentence I have just quoted the words 'nothing but' by 'to some extent' or 'from a certain angle' or 'on a certain level of his many-levelled structure', then everything is all right. The reductionist proclaims his part-truth to be the whole truth, a certain specific aspect of a phenomenon to be the whole phenomenon. To the behaviourist, the activities of man are *nothing but* a chain of conditioned responses; to the more rigid variety of Freudian, artistic creation is nothing but a substitute for goal-inhibited sexuality; to the mechanically oriented biologist the phenomena of consciousness are nothing but electrochemical reactions. And the ultimate reductionist heresy is to consider the whole as nothing but the sum of its parts – a hangover from the crude atomistic concepts of nineteenth-century physics, which the physicist himself abandoned long ago.

The second of the three Rs is what I have called elsewhere the philosophy of ratomorphism. At the turn of the century, Lloyd Morgan's famous canon warned biologists against the fallacy of projecting human thoughts and feelings into animals; since then, the pendulum has moved in the opposite direction, so that today, instead of an anthropomorphic view of the rat, we have a ratomorphic view of man. According to this view, our skyscrapers are nothing but huge Skinner boxes in which, instead of pressing a pedal to obtain a food-pellet, we emit operant responses which are more complicated, but governed by the same laws as the behaviour of the rat. Again, if you erase the 'nothing but', there is an ugly grain of truth in this. But if the life of man is becoming a rat-race, it is because he has become impregnated with a ratomorphic philosophy. One is reminded of that old quip: 'Psychoanalysis is the disease which it pretends to cure.' Keep telling a man that he is nothing but an oversized rat, and he will start growing whiskers and bite your finger.

Some fifty years ago, in the heyday of the conditioned reflex, the paradigm of human behaviour was Pavlov's dog salivating in its restraining harness on the laboratory table. After that came the rat in the box. And after the rat came the geese. In his recent book *On Aggression*, Konrad Lorenz advances the theory that affection between social animals is phylogenetically derived from aggression. The bond which holds the partners together (regardless of whether it has a sexual component or not) is 'neither more nor less than the conversion of aggression into its opposite'. Whether one agrees or disagrees with this theory is irrelevant; the reason why I mention it is that Lorenz's arguments are almost exclusively based on his observations of the so-called triumph ceremony of the greylag goose, which, in his own words, prompted him to write his book. Once more we are offered a *Weltanschauung* derived from an exceedingly specialized type of observations, a part-truth which claims to be the whole truth. To quote the Austrian psychiatrist, Viktor Frankl: 'The trouble is not that scientists are specializing, but rather that specialists are generalizing.'

A last example for the second R. About a year ago, a popular book on anthropology was heading the bestseller lists in Europe and America: *The Naked Ape: A Zoologist's Study of the Human Animal* by Dr Desmond Morris. It opens with the statement that man is a hairless ape 'self-named *homo sapiens* . . . I am a zoologist and the naked ape is an animal. He is therefore fair game for my pen.' To what extremes this zoomorphic approach may lead is illustrated by the following quotation:

The insides of houses or flats can be decorated and filled with ornaments, bric-a-brac and personal belongings in profusion. This is usually explained as being done to make the place 'look nice'. In fact, it is the exact equivalent to another territorial species depositing its personal scent on a landmark near its den. When you put a name on a door, or hang a painting on a wall, you are, in dog or wolf terms, for example, simply cocking your leg on them and leaving your personal mark there.

To avoid misunderstandings, let me emphasize once more that it is both legitimate and necessary for scientific research to investigate conditioned reflexes in dogs, operant responses in rats and the ritual dances of geese – so long as they are not forced upon us as paradigms for man's condition. But this is precisely what has been happening for the best part of our middle-aged century.

My third R is randomness. Biological evolution is considered to be nothing but random mutations preserved by natural selection; mental evolution nothing but random tries preserved by reinforcement. To quote from a textbook by a leading evolutionist: 'It does seem that the problem of evolution is essentially solved . . . It turns out to be basically materialistic, with no sign of purpose . . . Man is the result of a purposeless and materialistic process . . .'[2] To paraphrase Einstein, a non-existent God playing blind dice with the universe. Even physical causality, the solid rock on which that universe was built, has been replaced by the driftsands of statistics. We all seem to be in the condition which the physicist calls 'Brownian movement' – the erratic zigzag motions of a particle of smoke buffeted about by the molecules of the surrounding air.

Some schools of modern art, too, have adopted the cult of randomness. Action-painters throw at random fistfuls of paint at the canvas; a French sculptor achieved international fame by bashing old motor-cars with a demolition machine into random shapes; others assemble bits of scrap iron into abstract compositions, or bits of fluff and tinsel into collages; some composers of electronic music use randomizing machines for their effects. One fashionable novelist boasts of cutting up his typescript with a pair of scissors, and sticking it together again in random fashion.

These schools of contemporary art seem to derive their inspiration from the prevalent bias in the sciences of life – a kind of secondary infection. Randomness, we are told, is the basic fact of life. We live in a world crammed full with hard facts, and there is no place in it for purpose, values or meaning. To look for values and meaning is considered as absurd as it would be for an astronomer to search with his telescope for Dante's heavenly paradise. And it would be equally absurd to search with a microscope for that ghost in the machine, the conscious mind, with its ghostly attributes of free choice and moral responsibility.

Let us remind ourselves once more that the essence of teaching is not in the facts and data which it conveys, but in the interpretations that it transmits in explicit or implied ways. In terms of modern communication theory, the bulk of the information consists of interpretations. That is the core of the package: the data provide only the wrappings. But the recurrent, embittered controversies in the history of science prove over and over again that the same data can be interpreted in different ways and reshuffled into different patterns. A minute ago, I quoted a distinguished biologist of the orthodox neo-Darwinian school. Let me now quote another eminent biologist, C. H. Waddington, who, based on exactly the same available data, arrives at the opposite view: 'To suppose that the evolution of the wonderfully adapted biological mechanisms has depended only on a selection out of a haphazard set of variations, each produced by blind chance, is like suggesting that if we went on throwing bricks into heaps, we should eventually be able to choose ourselves the most desirable house.'[3]

One could go on quoting such diametrically opposed conclusions drawn by different scientists from the same body of data. For example, one could hardly expect neurophysiologists to belittle the importance of brain mechanisms in mental life, and many of them do indeed hold that mental life is nothing but brain mechanism. And yet Sherrington was an unashamed dualist; he wrote: 'That our being should consist of *two* fundamental elements offers, I suppose, no greater inherent improbability than that it should rest on one only.' And the great Canadian brain surgeon, Wilder Penfield, said at an interdisciplinary symposium on 'Control of the Mind' at which we both participated: 'To declare that these two things [brain and mind] are one does not make them so, but it does block the progress of research.'

I quote this, not because I am a Cartesian dualist – which I am not – but to emphasize that the neurophysiologist's precise data can be interpreted in diverse ways. In other words, it is not true that the data which science provides must automatically lead to the conclusion that life is meaningless, nothing but Brownian motion imparted by the random drift of cosmic weather. We should rather say that the *Zeitgeist* has a tendency to draw biased philosophical conclusions from the data, a tendency towards the devaluation of values and the elimination of meaning from the world around us and the world inside us. The result is an existential vacuum.

At this point I would like to quote again Viktor Frankl, founder of what has become known as the Third Viennese School of Psychiatry. He postulates that besides Freud's pleasure principle and Adler's will to power there exists a 'will to meaning' as an equally fundamental human drive:

It is an inherent tendency in man to reach out for meanings to fulfil and for values to actualize. In contrast to animals, man is not told by his instincts what he must do. And in contrast to man in former times, he is no longer told by his traditions and values what he ought to do ... Thousands and thousands of young students are exposed to an indoctrination along the lines of a

34

reductionist concept of life which denies the existence of values. The result is a world-wide phenomenon – more and more patients are crowding our clinics with the complaint of an inner emptiness, the sense of a total and ultimate meaninglessness of life.[4]

He calls this type of neurosis 'noogenic', as distinct from sexual and other types of neuroses, and he claims that about 20 per cent of all cases at the Vienna Psychiatry Clinic (of which he is the head) are of noogenic origin. He further claims that this figure is doubled among student patients of Central European origin, and that it soars to 80 per cent among students in the United States.

I should mention that I know next to nothing about the therapeutic methods of this school – it is called logotherapy – and that I have no means of judging its efficacy. But there exists a considerable literature on the subject, and I brought it up because the philosophy behind it seems to me relevant to our theme. However that may be, the term 'existential vacuum', caused by the frustration of the will to meaning, seems to be a fitting description of the worldwide mood of infectious restlessness, particularly among the young and among intellectuals.

It may be of some interest to compare this mood with that of the Pink Decade, the 1930s, when the Western world was convulsed by economic depression, unemployment and hunger marches, and the so-called Great Socialist Experiment initiated by the Russian Revolution seemed to be the only hopeful ideal to a great mass of youthful idealists, including myself. In *The God that Failed*, I wrote about that period:

Devotion to pure Utopia and rebellion against a polluted society are the two poles which provide the tension of all militant creeds. To ask which of the two makes the current flow – attraction by the ideal or repulsion by the social environment – is to ask the old question whether the hen was first, or the egg.

Compare this with the present mood. Today the repellent forces are more powerful than ever, but the attraction of the

35

ideal is missing, since what we thought to be Utopia turned out to be a cynical fraud. The egg is there, but no hen to hatch it. Rebellion is freewheeling in a vacuum.

Another comparison comes to mind – another historic situation, in which the traditional values of a culture were destroyed, without new values taking their place. I mean the fatal impact of the European conquerors on the native civilizations of American Indians and Pacific Islanders. In our case, the shattering impact was not caused by the greed, rapacity and missionary zeal of foreign invaders. The invasion has come from within, in the guise of an ideology which claims to be scientific and is in fact a new version of Nihilism in its denial of values, purpose and meaning. But the results in both cases are comparable: like the natives who were left without traditions and beliefs in a spiritual vacuum, we, too, seem to wander about in a bemused trance.

It is, of course, true that similar negative moods can be found in past periods of our history, variously described as *mal de siècle*, romantic despair, Russian Nihilism, apocalyptic expectations. And there have been Ranters, Messianic sects and Tarantula dancers, all of whom have their striking contemporary parallels. But the present has a unique and unprecedented urgency because the rate of change is now moving along an ever steeper exponential curve, and history is accelerating like the molecules in a liquid coming to the boil. There is no need to evoke the population explosion, urban explosion and explosion of explosive power; we live in their midst, in the eye of the hurricane.

This brings me back to my starting-point. The ideal of the educator as a catalysing agent is for the time being unattainable. Exceptions always granted, he has been a conditioning influence, and the conditions he created amount to an explosive vacuum.

I do not believe that the crisis in education can be solved by the educators. They are themselves products of that

Zeitgeist which brought on the crisis. All our laudable efforts to reform the universities can at best produce palliatives and symptom-therapy. I think that in a confused way the rebellious students are aware of this, and that this is why they are so helpless when asked for constructive proposals, and why no proposed reform can satisfy their ravenous appetites. They are, simply, hungry for meaning, which their teachers cannot provide. They feel that all their teachers can do is to produce rabbits out of empty hats. Up to a point the rebels have succeeded in imparting this awareness to society at large; and that, regardless of the grotesque methods employed, seems to me a wholesome achievement.

REFERENCES

1. *The Act of Creation* (London, 1964), pp. 265 *et seq.*
2. G. G. Simpson, *The Meaning of Evolution* (Newhaven, Conn., 1949).
3. In the *Listener*, 13 November 1952.
4. In *Beyond Reductionism: the Alpbach Symposium*, ed. A. Koestler and J. R. Smythies, (London, 1968).

Can Psychiatrists be Trusted?*

There are facts so obvious that one tends to overlook them. One of these facts is that the practice of medicine pre-dates the systematic study of physiology, and the practice of psychiatry pre-dates the systematic study of psychology. If we look back at the past, the physician appears as a figure levitating in mid-air, like an Indian Yogi, without any solid ground under his feet. The psychiatrist found himself in the same embarrassing situation, floating, as it were, on his fallible intuitions. At the somatic end of the psychosomatic spectrum – call it the infra-red end – the situation has been rapidly improving since biology started turning into an exact science; about infectious diseases at least we can do wonders. But at the ultra-violet end, where the psychiatric profession is operating, no comparable development is as yet in sight: academic psychology has failed to provide a solid foundation on which the levitating psychiatrist could rest his feet. He is faced with the responsibility of treating disorders of the mind without precise and reliable information about the processes which determine order in the mind. Pavlov's dogs, Skinner's rats and pigeons, Konrad Lorenz's geese have provided valuable analogies for certain simple aspects of human behaviour. But these analogies are of little use, and sometimes even an obstacle, to the understanding of the

* Paper read at the World Psychiatric Association Symposium on 'Uses and Abuses of Psychiatry', London, November 1969.

complex phenomena of language and language disorders; or of the storage and retrieval of memories and the pathology thereof.

Psycholonguistics, in the sense in which Chomsky and his school use this term, is a new branch of psychology which for the first time tries to come to grips with the problem how a child by the age of four has been able to acquire the immensely complex rules and strategies of language, how it can produce sentences it has never uttered before, understand sentences it has never heard before, and manipulate a syntactic and sematic machinery whose working is completely unknown to the child – as it is to the adult. For a century and more, academic psychology has not only failed to tackle this problem, but even to see the problem. But the neurosurgeon and psychiatrist has had his nose rubbed into it; and he had to try to make sense of the various bizarre types of aphasias and related disorders without getting any help from the psychologist. On the contrary, one might say with only a little exaggeration that it was neurosurgery that taught the psychologist what little real knowledge the latter has of the mechanisms of language and memory. Frederic Bartlett,[1] that great psychologist, got his immensely fruitful concept of the 'schema' from the neurologist, Henry Head; and the rather futile discussions about whether thinking consists of nothing but 'inner speech'. i.e., subliminal innervations of the vocal chords, or whether there is something more to it, would have continued *ad infinitum* had not clinical evidence of nominal or phonemic aphasia proved the existence of non-verbal types of mental activity. Penfield's electrode which made the patient mentally compare the drawing of a butterfly to a moth, without being able to recall either of the two words, has contributed more to the understanding of language than all the discussions of the introspectionists, behaviourists and Gestalt psychologists.[2] But it has been essentially a one-way traffic, and it still is.

Not only has academic psychology little help to offer to psychiatry, but its offerings have sometimes made confusion

39

worse confounded, as in the case of certain test procedures
based on specific models of memory – models which may give
a distorted picture of the patient's condition. Two years ago,
the late George Talland of the Harvard Medical School
organized an international symposium on '*The Pathology of
Memory*' in which I had the honour to participate – writers
are supposed to have a very peculiar sort of memory. While
the proceedings of the Symposium were being printed,
George Talland died. But the book has just come out,[3] and I
would like to quote a few passages from the memorable paper
that Talland read:

> Every psychologist who studies patients with memory defects
> tests them on one version or another of the immediate recall span.
> [However] we keep on rediscovering that men and women who
> barely remember an important incident that occurred last week
> can perform within normal limits on the standard digit span . . .
> Is the immediate retention span for unconnected items in fact at
> all relevant to normal memory function? . . . Patients with severe
> memory disorders do not perform much worse than healthy and
> normal people on these tests . . . A distinguished experimental
> psychologist . . . has on record the opinion that 'rote verbal
> learning is central to all human learning'. All the lessons I have
> learnt from a study of disturbed memory function force me to
> disagree with that opinion . . . Performance, the objective evi-
> dence that our behaviourist psychology relies on, often just skims
> the surface of a memory derangement and is apt to mislead us if
> it alone is admitted as evidence.

Talland then cites several cases of such misleading test-
results, and comments: 'These examples and others could be
listed to illustrate the inadequacy of the concepts employed
to evaluate acquisition and retention in verbal and other
experiments for the analysis of pathological disorders of
memory.' He ends by demanding a programme for experimental research on a more complex level, for designing tests
set up 'to test the accuracy of a clinical hunch' and for designing 'psychological models that fit the available models of
brain-function more closely than do most of those currently
in use'.

It is not difficult to detect behind these restrained formulations the anguish of the psychiatrist out on a limb. This predicament is, of course, most drastically reflected in the field of diagnosis and classification. As I seem to be the only outsider at this Congress of Psychiatrists, we must assume that I have been invited to represent that infernal nuisance in the psychiatrist's life, the patient. As a rule, of course, there are too many patients to one psychiatrist, whereas here the situation is reversed. But at the same time it reflects a different aspect of reality, for the single patient is potentially liable to be diagnosed and categorized in a great many different ways, depending to some extent on the psychiatric school, the ethnic background, and apparently even the age-group to which the diagnostician belongs. Thus, should I have the misfortune to be admitted to a mental hospital in England with a somewhat complex symptom-picture, I would have a ten-times higher chance of being classified as a manic depressive than if I were admitted to hospital in the United States; and taking my specific age-group into account, the ratio of United Kingdom to United States of patients diagnosed as manic depressives becomes 21 to 1. On the other hand, if I were to go off my head in America, I would stand a ten-times higher chance of being classified as a case of cerebral arterio-sclerosis than in England; and a 33 per cent higher chance of being classified as a schizo. In the States I might also be found to show a 'psychotic-depressive reaction', a category non-existent in England and Wales. I am quoting these figures from Morton Kramer's remarkable paper on 'A Cross-National Study of Diagnosis'.[4]

Nor could I, the patient, be more sure of what is wrong with me if you repeated on me the experiments of Martin Katz and associates – i.e., if you were to administer a psychiatric interview, which would be filmed and then shown to a number of experienced clinicians, asking them to arrive at a diagnosis based on a standard symptom-rating scale. Although I am sure you are familiar with the results, I may perhaps briefly refer to the data:[5]

In the first reported experiment, out of thirty-five American psychiatrists – 'all seasoned veterans', as Zubin[6] commented – fourteen diagnosed the patient as neurotic and twenty-one as psychotic. In another study, in which forty-two American psychiatrists participated, the patient, described as 'an attractive woman in her middle twenties', was classified by one third of the diagnosticians as schizophrenic, by another third as neurotic and by the third third as suffering from personality disorders. But when the same patient was diagnosed by British diagnosticians *not a single one* diagnosed her as schizophrenic, and 75 per cent diagnosed 'personality disorders'. On comparing the symptom rating by the British and American groups, it was discovered that the main cause of the contrast in diagnosis was that the Americans found in the patient very marked symptoms of apathy, while their British colleagues did not.

I repeat that I am sorry to go over this well-ploughed acre, not in order to rake up the dust, but because it suggests to one a simple and perhaps naïve hypothesis: could it be that psychiatrists, immersed in the bustling American world, are inclined to see apathy where their colleagues from this country only see placidity or British phlegm? The Americans also found considerable 'paranoid projection' and 'perceptual distortion' in the same patient in which the British found none of these symptoms. Could it be that psychiatrists in a highly conformist country read paranoid traits where the British see only idiosyncrasy or mild eccentricity?

However that may be, as Katz and his co-workers pointed out in their paper, these quantitative differences on the rating-scale lead to qualitatively different diagnoses – e.g., schizophrenia *versus* neurotic disorder – with all that this implies in terms of prognosis, hospitalization and therapy. If one remembers that one third of the American psychiatrists, *but not a single British psychiatrist*, pronounced the same patient schizophrenic, one is struck by another curious discrepancy. It is a well-known fact that in the United States a much higher proportion of well-to-do people keep what is called 'a tame analyst' than do their opposite numbers in this country. Is there a connection here with the cavalier attitude of American psychiatrists in diagnosing schizophrenia? Has the meaning of the term 'neurosis' been so widely stretched, or so watered-down, in the United States that if a patient shows signs of real trouble, as distinct from mere couch-addiction, nothing less than a diagnosis of psychosis will do?

These are speculations of a layman, but they make him feel fairly uncomfortable. In a recent paper, Joseph Zubin compared the clinical method of diagnosis, which he calls 'a creative act belonging to the realm of discovery' with the biometric approach, which

takes as its point of departure the objective measurement of the behaviour of the patient, applies taxonomic principles for classifying such behaviour, and finally appeals to statistical evaluation for determining the reliability and validity of a diagnostic label placed on the patient. Both approaches are essential since, without the clinician, there would be nothing to measure, and without measurements the clinician would soon become a prey to whatever wind of fashion blows.

The layman, of course, nods with solemn approval, yet with a touch of scepticism. The ambitious project which has recently got under way under the name of 'A Cross-National Study of Diagnosis of the Mental Disorders' will perhaps succeed in eliminating such drastic discrepancies in symptom-rating as I have just quoted; but it seems a Utopian hope that we shall ever be able to measure symptoms like 'apathy', 'hostile belligerence' or 'anxious intropunitiveness' with anything approaching the precision of measuring electrostatic charges. Biometrics strike one as a noble effort, but one wonders whether too much reliance on it cannot become self-defeating – and even whether it is not a contradiction in terms.

Which, in conclusion, brings me back to my starting-point,

43

and to George Talland's criticism of tests based on performance in rote learning and similar tasks. There seems to be no
getting away from the conclusion that, for the time being, the
psychiatrist's best friend is his intuition; and that he will only
feel solid earth under his feet when psychology grows out of
its obsession with rats in a maze and becomes a real science
of the human mind. But psychiatrists can continue to work
towards this goal by teaching their academic colleagues a
few of the facts of life.

REFERENCES

1. F. C. Bartlett, *Remembering* (Cambridge, 1961).
2. W. Penfield and L. Roberts, *Speech and Brain Mechanisms* (Princeton N. J., 1959).
3. Ed. Talland & Waugh, *The Pathology of Memory* (London, 1969).
4. *American Journal of Psychiatry*, Vol. cxxv, No. 10, April 1969, Supplement.
5. 'Studies of the Diagnostic Process', *American Journal of Psychiatry*, Vol, cxxv, No. 7, January 1969.
6. Biometric Assessment of Mental Patients' in *The Role and Methodology of Classification in Psychiatry and Psychopathology* (U.S. Department of Health, Education and Welfare, Public Health Service).

Life in 1980 – The Rule of Mediocracy*

A century ago, predicting developments fifty years ahead carried a smaller risk of making a fool of oneself than does attempting now to see five years ahead. History is accelerating at an unprecedented rate; the progress of a train ceases to be predictable when the brakes are off and the engine's overheating. On the other hand, there are always some stagnant enclaves which have an amazing power to survive virtually unchanged in the midst of the explosive flux. The obvious example is of course the British monarchy; it stays because, like Everest, it is there, though in contrast to Everest it tempts nobody to climb it; and it is a fairly safe bet that it will still be with us in the 1980s.

Another forecast one can venture with some confidence: regardless of whether we have a Labour, Tory or coalition government, we shall be ruled by a *mediocracy*. In Michael Young's meritocracy, merit was defined as I.Q. plus effort.

* In September 1969, as the decade was drawing to its close, *The Times* of London invited six members of different professions 'to try to forecast what life in 1980 will be like'. The following excursion into futurology appeared on 2 October 1969; subsequent contributors to the series were Sir Julian Huxley (on environment); J. K. Galbraith (on the superpower relationships); Herman Kahn (living with computers); Sir Bernard Lovell (space exploration) and Professor Asa Briggs (the growth of leisure).

45

In a mediocracy, on the other hand, the ingredients which define the successful mediocrat are common sense plus inertia. In the ideal mediocracy, towards which the country is progressing without unseemly haste, the term 'élite' becomes synonymous with 'average', and 'mediocre' with 'trustworthy'.

Explosive developments in the rest of the world may give rise to a new crop of Hitlers and Stalins, and the 1980s may easily turn into the Decade of the Demagogues. But not here. We shall more likely have a Decade of the Dentists, so called to commemorate the first member of that profession to become Prime Minister – a profession notoriously expert in depriving people of their bite. By way of compensation, the young will be encouraged to indulge in the cult of dottiness before they settle down and have their teeth pulled.

A third institutional enclave is also certain to survive: marriage and family. It has survived a couple of millennia, not because of its excellence – far from it – but because we have nothing else to put in its place without the risk of tearing the fabric of society to shreds. The Russians derided bourgeois marriage and ended up by tightening their divorce laws. The early kibbutzim in Palestine experimented with collective child-rearing and had to revert to the family structure. However, if the family remains the nucleus of society, it will, by the 1980s, have become even more radioactive, even more subject to fission, decay and splitting. To go through two or three marriages in a lifetime will be considered the norm, facilitated through divorce by consent. To marry without having previously been engaged in a trial affair will be considered irresponsible, considering the dangers of mistaking desire for affection, and the added risk of disillusionment; the term 'engaged to marry' will assume a new realistic meaning, and the period of engagement will be prolonged.

With the universal availability of the contraceptive pill for both sexes, the problems of abortion will lose its urgency. No woman will be coerced to give birth to an unwanted child; abortions will be performed without charge, but the irresponsible act of conceiving by negligence will entail a heavy fine, imposed without publicity.

Monogamy as an institution will thus continue to limp along with creaking joints; but at the same time, paradoxically, sex will have lost its sting, and guilt its victory. This does not imply unlimited promiscuity, but a sensible amount of it. The family unit will be preserved, but premarital and extramarital affairs will be taken for granted. With the waning of frustration and guilt, sex will continue to occupy a key position in literature and art, as it does in life; but after the mania for blue films and black novels has run its course, writers and film-makers will discover again that the implicit allusion is more effective than the explicit statement, and pubic hair less poetic than Gretchen's braids.

Education will have been revolutionized, but not on the university level. (In the student rebellions of the late 1960s the Alma Mater was merely the scapegoat for protests against the existential vacuum.) The breakthrough in education will have started in the mid 1970s, literally in the cradle, as a delayed reaction to the discoveries of American psychologists which were already available in the mid 1960s. Thus a research team in Berkeley had shown that rats exposed early after birth to a stimulating environment developed a thicker and more differentiated cerebral cortex than their litter mates reared in a poor and restricted milieu.[1] And the studies of Skeels and co-workers,[2] extending over a period of thirty years, revealed in a dramatic fashion that children who, around the age of twelve months, had been classified by conventional tests as mentally retarded, were transformed into slightly *above-average* adults by being transferred into an environment of optimal care and stimulation. The lesson that the growing mind is a voracious eater which has to be nourished from the cradle was slow to sink in, and it took even longer to overcome the resistance of educators refusing to distinguish between stimulation and conditioning. But when at long last the appropriate techniques were developed

47

and tested, the average child's intelligence began to rise to a level corresponding to the infant prodigies of earlier ages. The effects of the knowledge explosion were thus compensated to some extent; yet the little prodigies continued to enjoy the pleasures of childhood, such as weightless ping-pong and riding tame dolphins.

The Churches will also still be with us – de-mythologized, eviscerated, paying homage to gods that failed. Celibacy will have been abolished by a spirited papal decree including quotes from Rabelais; and after a dashing young priest got into the finals at Wimbledon, boxing and soccer will have become favourite pastimes of the modern type of clergyman. Signs of a universal secular ethics will still be nowhere in sight. Man remained a Janus-faced creature: a genius in mastering nature, a moron in conducting human affairs.

Turning to the material amenities of life, after the neurotic *au pair* the bane of the housewife's life will be the temperamental Bug – an insect-shaped robot, programmed every morning by punch-cards to scrub staircases, crawl up windows, exude polish, operate the washing-machine, open tins for lunch. Bugs will have a tendency to go berserk or indulge in a go-slow, and the Bug-repairman will display the same tendencies in more extreme form.

Traffic, after the growing chaos of the 1970s, will hold out hopes of improvement. These will be due to the wisdom of the London traffic-planners in putting a brilliant suggestion made by the present writer to the experimental test. Starting on T-Day on 1 January 1980, the Borough of Westminster was freed from the sight and sound of motor-cars. Instead, the residents found in the streets small electric runabouts, at every twenty yards or so, ready to be driven by anybody to any destination within the Borough, at a rate of ten pence per mile inserted into a slot in the instrument panel; the user could abandon the car wherever he liked. The experiment was such a success that it was soon extended to the whole of Greater London, and then to all large urban agglomerations in the country. Each borough had its collectively owned runabouts, marked by a distinctive colour, and not allowed out beyond its boundaries. A network of through roads mediated inter-borough traffic by normal cars, kept in garages at strategic points.

Traffic apart, people in the 1980s will move about much less. Entertainment by the mass media will be piped into every home. Ministries and office buildings will be made increasingly redundant by closed-circuit telecommunications systems, enabling civil servants, executives and their employees to conduct business from a desk in their suburban home. As screen-to-screen instead of face-to-face communications become the rule, curious neurotic symptoms will spread through the population, dubbed by psychiatrists as 'tactile deprivation'. Constant dialogues with three-dimensional screen-phantoms will create an irresistible urge to touch, buttonhole, punch or pat the disembodied appearance. However, ingenious devices called tactile simulators, together with tactile psychotherapy – 'touch what you see, paw what you like, *keep in touch*' – will help people not to lose entirely their 'grip' on reality.

To return to my starting-point: the difficulties of forecasting while history is accelerating like a jet before take-off. Three years ago, that excellent weekly the *New Scientist* invited about a hundred authorities of international repute in various fields to predict the state of affairs twenty years ahead – 'the world in 1984'. Amazingly, only four out of the hundred celebrities of this international brains trust referred to the possibility of a major war – and asserted that there would be none. The rest of them did not even mention the subject. I have followed their example, for what else can one do? The unimaginable cannot be spoken of.

In Büchner's *Danton* there is a scene in which the hero, having guessed that Robespierre is after him, spends a night hiding on a heath. It is cold and windy, so in the end he decides to go back home. Half his mind knows what is in store for him, but the other half cannot believe it. 'Whatever reason tells us,' he reflects, 'deep down in us there is a small smiling voice which says that tomorrow will be like yesterday.' A few hours later he is arrested.

It is the same voice which tells me that after lunch on 15 September 1980, I shall be hard at work on *The Times* Crossword Puzzle No. 15, 691.

REFERENCES

1. M. C. Diamond, E. Law, R. Rhodes, B. Lindner, M. R. Rosenzweig, D. Krech, E. L. Bennett, *Journal of Comparative Neurology*, Vol. CXXVIII, 1966, p. 177.
2. H. Skeels, *Monographs of the Society for Research in Child Development*, Vol. XXXI, No. 3, 1966.

Books in Review

Sins of Omission

While Six Million Died by Arthur D. Morse.*

Several years had to pass before the death of the six million, and the manner in which they were made to die, began to penetrate the mental defences of the West. It had the effect of a delayed shock, but at least there was the comforting thought that this had not been our doing, that we had no part in it, and no conceivable means of prevention or rescue.

This comfortable belief is no longer tenable. The evidence detailed in Mr Morse's book – mainly based on official State Department records which have not been published before – establishes with merciless clarity that a considerable proportion of the victims could have been saved; that men in responsible positions, in both the State Department and the Foreign Office, had been aware of the opportunities but had failed to make use of them, or even actively obstructed rescue attempts, for a variety of motives.

During the period 1933–9, from Hitler's ascent to power to the outbreak of war, it had become increasingly evident that the 700,000 Jews of Germany and Austria were doomed. The Nuremberg laws and other decrees had deprived them of their citizenship, excluded them from most professions, forced

* Reviewed in the *Observer*, 7 April 1968.

them to wear the yellow star, and imposed absolute racial segregation, while the concentration camps of Dachau and Buchenwald provided a foretaste of the later extermination camps. The only hope of survival was to emigrate, and only those who managed to do so did in fact survive.

At that stage, the Nazis were quite willing to let the Jews go, but the rest of the world was not willing to open its doors and admit more than a small, select proportion of the damned. In the first three years of the Nazi regime only 11,000 Jewish refugees were admitted into the United States, although the immigration quotas would have permitted the entry of 450,000 aliens and more than half of the places on the quota were unfilled. It was a deliberate consular practice of the period to enforce the immigration laws literally: thus Jews in hiding from the Gestapo were asked to produce police certificates from their home town in Germany attesting to their good character.

In March 1938, after the Nazi occupation of Austria and the wave of pogroms, mass arrests and mass suicides which followed it, the liberal forces in America demanded that the Administration take positive action. President Roosevelt had to do something, although he regarded (not without reason) 'the Jewish issue as a political liability': so he invited thirty-three governments to a conference in Evian-les-Bains 'to join in a co-operative effort to aid the immigration of refugees from Germany and Austria'. At the same time he declared at a Press reception that whatever the Conference decided, 'it would not result in an increase or revision of United States immigration quotas'.

The real purpose of the Evian Conference, as revealed by a confidential State Department memorandum of the time, was 'to get out in front and to attempt to guide the pressure, primarily with a view towards forestalling attempts to have the immigration laws liberalized' (p. 203). The other participants of the Conference were animated by the same spirit: 'One after another, the nations made clear their unwillingness to accept refugees. Since the business meetings were closed to the Press, they did not risk public exposure.' Australia, with vast unpopulated areas, announced : 'As we have no real racial problem, we are not desirous of importing one.' The Latin American countries struck the same note. The Peruvian delegate ironically remarked that the United States had given his country an example of 'caution and wisdom' by its own immigration restrictions. Only Holland and the Scandinavian countries showed their traditional humanitarianism and sense of responsibility; but they could absorb only drops from the potential flood. A British delegate reported that 'the British Colonial Empire contained no territory suitable to the large-scale settlement of refugees'. Dr Weizmann, President of the Jewish Agency, was refused a hearing; and 'his Majesty's delegation, led by Lord Winterton, managed to evade the delicate subject of the Jewish National Home in Palestine for the duration of the Conference'.

That infamous conference was a symbol of an age: it revealed the bankruptcy of humanitarianism as Munich revealed the bankruptcy of political ethics. Moreover, it served as an indirect encouragement to the German Government to carry out its extermination policies without fear of too much antagonism from the rest of the world. Hitler commented with glee: 'We are ready to put all these criminals at the disposal of these countries, for all I care, even on luxury ships. But nobody wants them.'

So much for the prewar period. One might be inclined to believe that once the war had started there were no further opportunities of rescue; but this view is mistaken. Although the underground chambers at Auschwitz were each capable of gassing 2,000 tightly packed people in twenty-five minutes, and the forty-six ovens were capable of burning 500 bodies per hour, the Nazis were not quite able to finish the job by the end of the war. The gas chambers were located in Eastern Europe; they had to find, collect and transport the six million from all over Europe, from France, Scandinavia, the Balkans; and the dragnet worked slowly and erratically, often encountering passive or active resistance in occupied and satellite countries.

Under these circumstances there existed many avenues of rescue. Three of the most important were escape to a neutral nation, hiding in occupied countries, and allied pressure on satellite governments. Three examples from Mr Morse's book may serve to illustrate how these opportunities were used.

In April 1943, neutral Sweden was ready to request that Germany release 20,000 Jewish children, who would be cared for in Sweden until the end of the war, provided that the United States and Britain would guarantee to provide a haven for them after the war. The State Department blocked the proposal under various pretexts for eight months, by which time relations between Sweden and Germany had so deteriorated that it was too late.

Also in April 1943, the so-called Riegner plan proposed the transfer of Jewish charity funds to the underground in France, to be used for the rescue of children from the concentration camps in the south and to expedite the departure to Spain and North Africa of those in hiding. It again took eight months – from April to December 1943 – until permission was granted to transfer $25,000 to France in the face of strenuous opposition from the State Department. According to the Abbé Glasberg, one of the organizers of the action, 'he and his colleagues could have saved virtually all of the 60,000 Jewish victims of the Nazis in France if they had possessed two weapons – American visas and more money'.

One last example. During 1941 and 1942, the Fascist Government of Marshal Antonescu had deported 185,000 Romanian Jews to camps in Transnistria, where conditions equalled those in Auschwitz. By early 1943 100,000 of them had perished. After the battle of Stalingrad, Antonescu began to fear an Allied victory and offered to transfer the surviving 70,000 Jews to any refuge selected by the Allies. A Red Cross delegation which had visited Romania reported that the evacuation could take place 'at once if the necessary funds were available'. The State Department and Foreign Office between them blocked the project for nearly a whole year. By then out of 185,000 only 48,000 were left.

The appointment of the War Refugee Board in January 1944 put an end to the State Department's obstructionist policy; its remarkable achievements demonstrated what could have been done during the wasted years. But by that time four million out of the six were dead.

Mr Morse's book spells out the facts without attempting to analyse the motives behind them. They form a complex tangle of unconscious prejudices, cynical expediency and spurious rationalizations. Among the latter were, in prewar days, such utterances as 'the treatment of German citizens is an internal affair of Germany', 'protests can only aggravate the situation', and so on; and during the war, 'shortage of shipping' (American troop transports to Europe often returned empty), 'rescue operations would impede the war effort'; and above all, 'we must not single out a particular religious group for preferential treatment' (an earlier variant of Ernest Bevin's classic remark, 'the Jews should not push to the head of the queue').

When, in 1939, a Bill was introduced in the United States Senate asking for the admission of 20,000 refugee children under the age of fourteen in addition to the German quota, the Secretary of State, Cordell Hull, objected that this would 'inevitably necessitate increased clerical personnel as well as additional office accommodation'. The American Legion had another objection: 'it is traditional American policy that home life should be preserved, and the American Legion therefore strongly opposes the breaking up of families, which would be done by the proposed legislation'. A representative of the Widows of World War I Veterans described the prospective immigrants under fourteen as 'thousands of motherless, embittered, persecuted children of undesirable foreigners, and potential Communists'.

Two public polls summed up the nation's state of mind. Early in 1939 a Gallup poll revealed that 94 per cent of the American people disapproved of the German treatment of the Jews. A few months later, when the Bill about the children was being debated, *Fortune* magazine organized another poll including the question: 'If you were a member of Congress, would you approve a Bill to open the doors to a larger number of refugees than now admitted under our quotas?' Eighty-three per cent said no. The Bill was never passed.

President Roosevelt had to manœuvre an isolationist Congress and public and, as he remarked to Mrs Roosevelt, 'first things come first'. Expediency carried the day – or was it the century? – as it did for different reasons in the Vatican, in England, and in a number of other democracies vaunting their humanitarian traditions. But we must face the ugly and challenging fact that it was the voice of the people, both inside Germany and among her opponents, which carries the ultimate responsibility for the fate of the six million.

The Future, if any

The Biological Time-Bomb by Gordon Rattray Taylor*

In 1963 Dr R. J. White's research team at Cleveland, Ohio, succeeded in removing a monkey's brain from its skull and keeping it alive on artificial circulation for seven hours. Proof that it was alive was provided by the brain's electrical and chemical activity. Soon afterwards, three Wisconsin surgeons repeated the experiment on fifteen dogs. Then the Cleveland team went one better; they removed the entire heads of dogs and connected them to the circulation of other dogs. The transplanted heads were reported to have stayed alive several days; their eyes contracted when light was shone into them, and there was a 'rhythmic gasping'.

Were the heads conscious? In Dr White's opinion consciousness cannot exist without bodily sensations, and since the nervous pathways had been cut, 'consciousness as we know it was unlikely to occur'. Many psychologists would disagree with this view. At a television interview the surgeon was asked whether human brains, too, could be kept alive by the same technique. He replied: 'There is no question that this is within the capacities of laboratories today.' He

* Reviewed in the *Observer*, 21 April 1968.

59

added that it would even be easier than with monkeys and dogs because we have more sophisticated heart and lung machines for humans than for animals.

The rationale of the experiments is that they will benefit surgery on patients with damaged brains. They certainly will; but there is little doubt that the same beneficial results could be obtained by less blasphemous methods. Dr White must surely be aware of this; and although he assured his television viewers that he personally would not attempt to keep disembodied human brains alive because of the 'social implications' [*sic*], one suspects that the conscious or unconscious motivation behind the experiments is precisely the search for this kind of obscene immortality. Nor will there be a lack of buyers for it.

Gordon Rattray Taylor is one of our best popularizers of science. In his present book, he demonstrates convincingly that biology is just reaching the critical point of sudden acceleration which physics reached a generation ago. While we are still punch-drunk and reeling from the impact of the technological revolution, the biological time-bomb is about to explode in our face.

Actually, the explosion has already started, though most of us are unaware of it. Artificial insemination of women and cattle has been a routine for some years, and sperm banks are already in existence. Dr Behrman of Michigan University has produced healthy children by injecting sperm which has been frozen for two-and-a-half years, and procreation by the dead will soon become commonplace. The converse procedure is artificial inovulation: the fertilized eggs of a prize-winning cow are implanted into the wombs of cows of a lesser breed, where they are brought to term. Thus ovum banks will soon be added to the sperm banks. The next step is to bring eggs and sperm together in test-tubes, and to implant the fertilized egg into the uterus. This method has so far only been tried on pigs, but Dr R. G. Edwards of Cambridge, who did these experiments, is confident that 'we may shortly obtain (by this method) human embryos in the process of cleaving'. The final step is the Baby Factory in *Brave New World*, where the entire development, from fertilization to finished product, is achieved *in vitro*. Experts believe that this will become possible by the end of the century. By that time, of course, such minor problems as choice of sex in the offspring will long have been solved.

By that time also, a revolutionary method of reproducing organisms will have become practicable; a method which excludes the hazards of genetic variation and guarantees to produce an unlimited number of offspring which are exact duplicates in every respect of a single parent, male or female. The method is called 'cloning' (or popularly, 'people from cuttings'), and consists essentially in techniques to derive offspring from an *adult* cell, not an embryonic cell, in the body of the parent (the nucleus of the adult cell transplanted into an enucleated egg regains its genetic potential and produces a xerox copy, so to speak, of the animal). To date, the technique has only been demonstrated in frogs; but the author quotes a number of leading physiologists to the effect that cloning 'holds out the possibility, *right away*, of producing exact copies of prize bulls, race-winning horses or exceptional human beings . . . As one commentator observed, compared with the ethical problems raised, the scientific ones are trivial.' The consequences of such biological xeroxing of armies or praetorian guards for a totalitarian dictatorship need not be spelled out.

Among the less sensational developments to be expected during the lifetime of the present generation of teenagers are extension of the lifespan and raising of the I.Q. level. A recent study on current trends in research, in which eighty-two experts participated, worked out a kind of timetable of the future. They forecast that by A.D. 2012 about fifty years will have been added to the average life expectancy, and that by A.D. 2050 (Rattray Taylor thinks much earlier) there will be an indefinite prolongation of the lifespan by inducing quasi-hybernatory states of suspended animation (lowering of the rate of metabolism). They do not tell us what the outcome

61

of the population explosion combined with a lifespan explosion might be.

As for the boosting of intelligence in animals and man, there are at present several experimental approaches. These include the administration of hormones to the pregnant mother (Zamenhof), providing the foetus with an added oxygen supply (Heyn's decompression treatment), and providing optimal environmental conditions for the newborn (Krech and Bennett). As a by-product of these endeavours we may expect the breeding, or cloning, of animals with superior intelligence to replace human labour. The eighty-two experts put the date at 2050.

On the hopeful side we are promised that by New Year's Eve, 1999, physical pain will be a bad memory of the past; on the other hand, there are the unlimited possibilities of biological warfare, fought by mutated viruses instead of soldiers, and nerve-gas clouds instead of bombs. Fortunately, where imagination gives out there is no room left for fear.

But imagination responds only too vividly to another development: genetic engineering. Since Crick and Watson succeeded in breaking the genetic code, geneticists all over the world have started to tamper with it. One prominent biochemist, Professor Joshua Lederberg, believes that we shall soon be able 'to implant human cell nuclei into animals, perhaps apes, and thus produce hybrids'; and that these experiments will be 'pushed in steps as far as biology will allow'.

How far is that? One possible development among many others is that hybridization, combined with organ transplantation and the raising of intelligence, might create a new type of industrial proletariat:

> The experiment of transferring human limbs to an animal may well be tried . . . For the tasks of a technological civilization hands with fingers which can press buttons are required, and an opposable thumb is needed for many types of operation. It would therefore be logical to equip apes with discarded human hands . . . The ultimate phase will be cross-species cannibalization: the

attachment of simian arms and a dog's head to a kangaroo, for instance, might create a creature capable of covering huge distances fast and doing a skilled job when it gets there . . . Dogs with two heads have already been created in Russia some time ago. For an athlete a supplementary heart might well be useful . . . Within a few years we may actually see such chimeras . . . If it is profitable to make man-animal chimeras, we shall make them.

But man does not live by profit alone, and some genetic engineers may have an artistic temperament; thus there is hope that fifty years from now there will be centaurs capering through Kensington Gardens, and mermaids offering cups of tea to sailors on the Serpentine, while goaty Pan will blow his pipe under the Albert Memorial in an aerosol cloud of deodorant. For this is the point where we give up and the shudders give way to the giggles. Even if logic tells us that most of these predictions will come true, imagination stalls; we cannot project ourselves into the future twenty-five years ahead any more than into the pre-Copernican past 500 years back. In the accelerating flow of time the two distances are about the same.

Going Down the Drain

The Doomsday Book by Gordon Rattray Taylor*

This is not a book about the dying panda, smog over the cities and oil on the beaches. They have shrunk to trivial episodes in a global tragedy, in which we all participate as actors or chorus without being aware of it. *The Doomsday Book* is an attempt to convey that awareness by tracing the plot and analysing its tangled causes. Before I read it I thought I knew most of the essential facts; when I had finished I marvelled at my previous state of ignorance.

In his introductory chapter Rattray Taylor has two striking analogies, which seem to define the boundaries of the predicament:

> Put bacteria in a test-tube, with food and oxygen, and they will grow explosively, doubling in number every twenty minutes until they form a solid, visible mass. But finally multiplication will cease as they become poisoned by their own waste products. In the centre of the mass will be a core of dead and dying bacteria cut off from the food and oxygen of their environment . . . Mankind today is in a similar position. The pollutants which poison our air and water . . . pose a threat to life precisely because man's growth has been so abnormally rapid.

* Reviewed in the *Sunday Times*, 6 September 1970.

The second analogy is meant to explode the belief that the earth is a world with unlimited supplies of air, water, sunshine, animals, plants, minerals, forests and fertile soil; however much of them man uses up, nature will replace it. This belief, once justified, has ceased to be so:

The fact is, we are just beginning to press up against the limits of the earth's capacity . . . The realization has dawned that earth is a spaceship with strictly limited resources. These resources must in the long run be recycled either by nature or by man. Just as the astronaut's urine is purified to provide drinking water and just as his expired air is regenerated to be breathed anew, so all the earth's resources must be recycled sooner or later. But the margins are getting smaller. All we have is a narrow band of usable atmosphere no more than seven miles high, a thin crust of land only one eighth of the surface of which is really suitable for people to live on, and a limited supply of drinkable water which we continually re-use . . . These resources are tied together in a complex set of transactions. We heedlessly intervene in these transactions.

These 'heedless interventions' provide the leitmotiv of the tragedy. But even if ignorance were miraculously replaced by wisdom, it is doubtful whether the catastrophe could still be prevented *unless* – and this is the central thesis of the book – two seemingly Utopian conditions are fulfilled: reversing the population growth and putting a stop to the advances of technology.

The majority of scientists, industrialists, planners and administrators do not share this view. They will react to this book with accusations of hysteria and the usual soothing noises. Even scientists who have given serious thought to the problem and realize that all is not well incline to the view that the symptoms which make life increasingly unliveable are merely by-products of Progress – comparable to the tiresome side-effects of antibiotics. But this view seems to be no longer tenable. Rattray Taylor demonstrates, to my mind convincingly, that the deterioration of the quality of human life is an *unavoidable* consequence of the combination of two factors: (a) the sudden explosive proliferation of our species;

(b) the equally explosive increase of its power to exploit and plunder the environment – not with evil intent, but driven by the force of circumstances.

What drives one to this conclusion is a new insight into the delicacy and vulnerability of those self-regulating processes which maintain the ecological equilibrium on all levels – from the planet's climate down to the corals of the Great Barrier Reef and down to the micro-fauna in a person's guts. Because of this precarious balance, a small external disturbance may throw the whole complex system of interlocking processes out of gear, or trigger off a chain reaction. But if this is so, then factors (a) and (b) mentioned in the previous paragraph may have a more brutal and dangerous impact on the whole biosphere of our planet than was generally assumed. What we thought of as mere pinpricks inflicted on it now look more like lethal injuries.

Take climate. During the last Ice Age, which killed off the last of our Neanderthal cousins, the mean temperature is estimated to have been only 5 to 8 degrees Centigrade below the present average. Moreover, some of the major climatic changes seem to have been remarkably abrupt – witness the many specimens of quick-frozen mammoths standing on their feet with bits of grass between their teeth, presumably caught and buried in a blizzard which was followed by no thaw. The multiple factors which trigger off these slow or rapid changes are as yet hardly known; but the technological explosion has enabled us to tamper unwittingly with the thermostatic controls of the planet. Even pre-industrial man changed the climate of whole sub-continents by deforestation, turning fertile land into desert; today we are in the process of obliterating the sun – not only over smog-bound cities but on a global scale. On the island of Mauna Loa, Hawaii, which is far from any industrialized area, 'atmospheric turbidity' (haze) has increased (in ten years) by 30 per cent. In Davos, on the Magic Mountain, it has increased (since 1930) by 80 per cent. In the Caucasus, over the same period, by a remarkable 1900 per cent.

The fine particles of gases belched into the sky by chimneys and exhaust pipes are lusty travellers who love the fresh air. During the war, quantities of dust fell over the Caribbean isles which had been stirred up by the tank battles in North Africa. A powerful boost to increased cloud formation is provided by the condensation trails of jet planes. It is estimated that the cloud-cover over the North Atlantic is already 10 per cent above normal. With the coming of supersonic transport 'it is probable that long before the turn of the century the Atlantic, together with much of North America and Europe, will be permanently under cloud'. The blue sky will be a yarn told by oldsters.

Turbidity has also the effect of reflecting the sun's heat, so that less of it reaches the earth. One British expert, Dr Jim Lovelock, predicted the start of a new Ice Age 'well before 1980'. Other scientists predict an equally catastrophic *rise* in temperature within a few decades, owing to the increase of carbon dioxide in the atmosphere and the heat which industry discharges into it. Nobody knows for certain how this complex system with its positive and negative feedbacks works; we manipulate the controls of Spaceship Earth without being informed what the buttons are for.

'It is estimated that more than a quarter million different substances are released as wastes, effluents or gases. Practically none of them have been tested for their possible effects on the ecosphere.' But now the effects are beginning to make themselves felt. Fish in Sweden are discovered to carry 'up to a lethal 101 p.p.m. (parts per million) of mercury, fifty times the normal amount'. This is one example of a sinister mechanism called 'biological concentration'. Scottish trout, fed on brine shrimp larvae specially imported from the Great Salt Lake, died because each shrimp carried a small amount of pesticides which had got into the lake – not enough to kill the shrimp but enough to kill the trout after it had eaten a few hundred shrimps. Cows accumulate radioactive iodine in their thyroids; oysters and shellfish accumulate fall-out; and as for humans, the author sums up his detailed survey of the Great Pesticide Controversy with the lapidary statement that 'the milk of American mothers contains so much D.D.T. that it should not be given to babies'. The major rivers of Europe and North America are polluted; the great and small lakes are dying or dead; even fish in the oceans cannot escape the choice menu of poisons going down the drains. The Sorcerer's Apprentice is no longer a cliché, but has grown into an archetype.

These are only a few glimpses of *The Doomsday Book*'s rigorously documented collection of data. In his last chapter the author tries to sound an optimistic note, but does not quite succeed. Instead of a sermon he ends with a murmured 'it is the future of the human race that we have been talking about'.

Benighted Attitudes

The Biocrats by Gerald Leach*

Some of my best friends are gynaecologists, but I could not help my blood-pressure going up when I read this piece of information in Gerald Leach's book (his italics):

> A recent survey of Fellows of the Royal College of Gynaecologists found that 192 were opposed to *any* form of abortion on 'social' grounds and only 5 were for it.

The same attitude prevails in the medical profession in general, in the legal profession, in the Churches. A permissive society is not necessarily an enlightened society. Ours is permissive because it has no other choice left; tolerance has been extorted under duress, but it lacks spontaneity and insight. It has swallowed the Pill with grudging reluctance, it has abolished the gallows under hysterical protests, but when it comes to controversial questions such as euthanasia or abortion, the professional establishment displays the same benighted attitudes as the uninformed man in the street.

The law on abortion has been liberalized but, as Leach tells us, 'a year after the 1968 Abortion Act was passed only one abortion in five – about 40,000 out of an estimated

---

* Reviewed in the *Observer*, 26 April 1970.

200,000 a year – was done under good medical supervision. The other 160,000 were done by women on themselves or by back-street operators.' There is still a strong opprobrium attached to terminating pregnancy, and the machinery of obtaining medical or psychiatric approval is so intimidating that most women cannot face it 'and prefer to go down the street rather than confront society's well-dressed, inquisitive watchdogs'.

As long as contraception remains fallible, 'women will go on seeking and getting abortions rather than having to bear children they do not want. They will do this whatever the law of the land, the medical profession or anyone else says about it. And contrary to popular opinion, most of them will not be 'reckless' unmarried girls but 'respectable' married women – for the simple reason that most women of child-bearing age are married . . . Restrictive abortion laws made a mockery of the dignity of the law. Since these laws cannot suppress abortions, they merely ensure that most abortions are illegal.'

In a carefully documented chapter, Leach shows that the medical and psychological risks attached to terminating pregnancy under proper surgical care are largely imaginary, whereas the risks of coercing women to give birth to an unwanted child are shockingly real. He quotes a Swedish study – the first of its kind – of 120 children who were born after their mothers had asked for and been refused an abortion. The development of these children was followed up to their twenty-first birthday. Result: twice as many of them had psychiatric trouble as the normal average; twice as many of them had a record of juvenile delinquency; seven times as many of them required public assistance after sixteen. If we turn from rich, enlightened Sweden to a less privileged country such as Colombia, we find that nearly half of all the women in hospital are there because of botched abortions 'and if abortion fails, there is always infanticide. Many women are underfeeding their children, letting them get sick, throwing them outside the house, and then taking

70

them to the doctor knowing it is too late.' Infanticide is apparently more acceptable than foeticide to the watchdogs of society.

Even in Italy and some other Western European countries it is estimated that the number of illegal abortions equals that of live births. Leach suggests that the only realistic solution would be to legalize abortion 'on demand', without any strings attached. He hopes that the resistance of the clerical and professional establishments will be finally broken down by the invention of a safe abortion pill (not to prevent but to terminate unwanted pregnancy). He concludes:

Technical innovations have shattered apparently immutable moral truths before. And with the abortion pill they may well do so again. I cannot believe that we will not be the better for it . . . Human beings will at least have within their grasp the power to make their own private decisions about controlling their fertility. That would be a very great victory for personal freedom.

Science reporters are supposed to take a neutral attitude on controversial issues, and to convey their personal bias in coyly oblique ways. Leach sticks his neck out. He argues that the breathtaking advances in biological medicine require an equally radical re-valuation of our system of values and order of priorities. And indeed, what is the point of repeating like an opera chorus that the sorcerer's apprentices should be brought under the wise control of 'society', if society – the Minister of Health? the Vatican? the media? – is quite unable to comprehend what is going on in the sorcerer's laboratory, let alone to 'control' it? So one must try to make the mass of the people conscious of these goings-on, before it is too late. That is why books like *The Biocrats* or Rattray Taylor's *The Biological Time-Bomb* or the earlier warnings of Rachel Carson are so important. Government measures against pollution are grotesquely inadequate, the Auschwitz done on the fishes goes merrily on, and in the larger part of the globe populations are exploding straight into starvation. But at least people are beginning to talk; whereas ten years ago warnings about the impending biological crisis were shrugged off, it has now become a topical subject, and growing awareness is bound to lead to growing protests against our passive drift towards collective misery and the degeneration of the species.

In keeping with the book's purpose, the author explains in his preface that it 'covers few ventures into the future more than a decade or so ahead. The technical future is coming at us very fast and is almost completely obscure beyond a ten-year or at most fifteen-year time-span.'

This is justified caution, for extrapolations further ahead inevitably transform futurology into science fiction. The latter has its charms, but little to offer in the way of solutions for the immediate social problems triggered off by each biological advance. It does not help much to be told that in 1994 the first man-ape chimeras will go on their first wildcat strike – to coin a hybrid metaphor.

Lastly, the author has some courageous things to say against a 'Christian ethic, which holds that even the near-vegetable Cyclops-child with its one eye in its forehead has an inviolable right to live'. We get some glimpses of 'hospitals for sub-normal children where incontinent idiots literally wallow in their own excrement', and he comes down, by implication, in favour of the mercy killing of babies born as hopeless monsters. But it is a pity that he does not discuss euthanasia in the equally hopeless terminal diseases of adults. For this is one of the fields in which the need for the re-valuation of our values is obvious. In large parts of the world modern death control without birth control has produced catastrophic results. But the new methods of prolonging life by sophisticated artifices can also be catastrophic for the moribund individual in intractable pain. Paradoxically, we find that a great many of those politicians, lawyers and doctors who were in favour of retaining capital punishment are rigidly opposed to abortion and euthanasia – in the name of the sanctity of life. To kill an embryo before it has gained consciousness, to terminate, mercifully, hopeless suffering is sinful; to break mercilessly a man's neck is apparently not. Logic is a many-splendoured thing.

The Naked Touch

Intimate Behaviour by Desmond Morris*

In the Introduction to his previous bestseller, *The Naked Ape*, Desmond Morris declared: 'I am a zoologist and the naked ape is an animal. He is therefore fair game for my pen.'

The opening sentences of the present book are no less provocative:

> The act of intimacy occurs whenever two individuals come into bodily contact. It is the nature of this contact, whether it be a handshake or a copulation, a pat on the back or a slap in the face, a manicure or a surgical operation, that this book is about . . . My method has been that of the zoologist trained in ethology, that is, in the observation and analysis of animal behaviour (p. 9).

In *The Naked Ape* this 'zoological approach' yielded some revealing, or at least amusing, sidelights on the evolutionary origin of certain human traits and social rites. *Intimate Behaviour* offers hardly any such rewards, except perhaps in the first chapter, which emphasizes the newborn infant's need for bodily contact with the mother as a partial substitute for the previous 'intra-uterine bliss'. The next two chapters – 'Invitations to Sexual Intimacy' followed, as you would

* Reviewed in the *Observer*, 10 October 1971.

expect, by 'Sexual Intimacy' – read like an involuntary pastiche of the genre:

Since their reappearance, the naked navels of the Western world have undergone a curious modification. They have started to change shape. In pictorial representations, the old-fashioned circular aperture is tending to give way to a more elongated, vertical slit. Investigating this odd phenomenon, I discovered that contemporary models and actresses are six times more likely to display a vertical navel than a circular one, when compared with the artist's models of yesterday. A brief survey of two hundred paintings and sculptures showing female nudes, and selected at random from the whole range of art history, revealed a proportion of 92 per cent of round navels to 8 per cent of vertical ones. A similar analysis of pictures of modern photographic models and film actresses shows a striking change: now the proportion of vertical ones has risen to 46 per cent . . . How this change has come about . . . is not entirely clear. The ultimate significance of the new navel shape is, however, reasonably certain. The classical round navel, in its symbolic orifice role, is rather too reminiscent of the anus. By becoming a more oval, vertical slit, it automatically assumes a much more genital shape, and its quality as a sexual symbol is immensely increased (p. 41).

After the navel, the breasts. These are 'more than a mere feeding device', and 'can better be thought of as another mimic of a primary sexual zone; in other words, as biologically developed copies of the hemispherical buttocks. This gives the female a powerful sexual signal when she is standing vertically, in the uniquely human posture, and facing a male' (p. 52).

The style is, as it were, touching:

The belly. Moving up above the genital region now, we come to the belly, which has two characteristic shapes: flat and 'pot'. Lovers tend to be flat-bellied, while pot-bellies are most commonly seen in starving children and overfed men (p. 47).

Moving up even further now, 'eye movements of various kinds also invite intimacy. Apart from the well-known wink, the rolling of the eyes is also reported to be a direct invitation to copulation in certain cultures. A demure dropping of the eyes also transmits its message in the female, while a slight narrowing of them can indicate interest on the part of the male' (p. 64).

An extreme form of intimacy is the rape:

> For the human male animal, rape is comparatively easy. If physical force is not enough, he can add threats of death or injury. Alternatively he can contrive to render the female unconscious or semi-unconscious, or can enlist the aid of other males to hold her still. If the absence of the female's sexual arousal makes penis insertion difficult or painful, he can always resort to the use of some alternative form of lubrication to replace the missing natural secretions (p. 80).

The particular flavour of the modern, pseudo-scientific sex-pot-boiler is a kind of salacious pedantry, and Dr Morris, however serious his intentions, has not altogether succeeded in avoiding it. One is almost relieved when the pedantry gains the upper hand:

> All animal courtship patterns are organized in a typical sequence, and the course taken by a human love affair is no exception. For convenience we can divide the human sequence up into twelve stages, and see what happens as each threshold is successfully passed (p. 74).

The twelve stages listed and discussed are: (1) eye to body, (2) eye to eye, (3) voice to voice, (4) hand to hand, (5) arm to shoulder, (6) arm to waist, (7) mouth to mouth, (8) hand to head, (9) hand to body, (10) mouth to breast, (11) hand to genitals, (12) genitals to genitals. There are also variations, which 'take three main forms: a reduction of the sequence, an alteration in the order of the acts and an elaboration of the pattern' (p. 79).

After 'Sexual Intimacy' we pass to 'Social Intimacy', i.e., restrained, inhibited or symbolic bodily contacts, such as clapping – 'When we applaud a performer, we are, in effect, patting him on the back from a distance' – and waving one's hand as a welcome or farewell sign. But there are also 'two rather specialized waves' singled out for discussion: 'the Papal wave and the British Royal wave'.

From 'Social Intimacy' we move to 'Specialized Intimacy' with 'professional touchers' such as 'the doctor, the nurse, the masseur, the gymnastics and health-and-beauty instructors, the hairdresser, the tailor, the manicurist, the beautician, the make-up specialist, the barber, the shoeshine and the shoe-shop attendant. To this list we could add many other related occupations such as those of the wigmaker, the hatter, the chiropodist, the dentist, the surgeon, the gynaecologist' (p. 158).

The next chapter discusses intimacy with pets, which Morris decrees to be 'living substitutes for human bodies in a contact-hungry world'. We are informed that 'at a rough guess, there are approximately 150 million cats and dogs in these four countries alone [United States, France, West Germany and Britain]. Making another rough guess, let us say that each owner of one of these animals strokes, pats or caresses it, on the average, three times a day – or about 1,000 times a year. This adds up to a total of 150,000 million intimate body contacts per year' (p. 173).

Next, we are treated to a ten-page dissertation on vivisection, which the author manages to drag in under the pretext that it represents a 'betrayal of intimacy'. Similarly, there is a discussion of the horrors of lung cancer, justified by the remark that cigarettes are substitutes for intimate contact with the nipple and 'warm inhaled smoke equals mother's warm milk'.

Lastly we have 'Self-Intimacy', from masturbation to the various ways of touching one's head or face with one's hand. 'Surveying these head contacts it was possible to identify 650 different types of action. This was done by recording which part of the hand was used, how it made the contact, and which part of the head was involved' (p. 215).

The Germans have a word for it: *Die Wissenschaft des nicht Wissenswerten* – the science of what is not worth knowing. After a number of highly enjoyable books on snakes, pandas and apes – including the naked one – Dr Morris this time has indulged in filling a rag-bag with miscellaneous bits of information which add little to our knowledge of human nature, but makes it appear in a crude and grotesquely distorted shape; while the author's reflections on why we pet pets and feel what we touch strike one as tautologies wrapped in truisms. As for his central thesis – shared by certain group-encounter cults of Californian origin – that modern man is frustrated in his need of intimate body contacts, the fairest verdict is: not proven – and one might even plausibly argue that just the opposite is true.

Not by Hate Alone

Love and Hate by Irenaus Eibl-Eibesfeldt*

Like the 'Believe It or Not' cartoons, this book is full of
recondite bits of information. For instance:

Amongst the Dama in South Africa the parting blessing uttered
by an adult person runs: 'May you be wetted upon by the fathers,
my uncles!' . . . Rites actually involving urine occur among the
Hottentots. If a man has killed a lion, an elephant or a rhinoceros,
his heroic deed is celebrated in the following way: he retires to
his hut until an old man fetches him out of the kraal and invites
him to come and be honoured. He leads him to the centre of the
village where all the men are gathered, waiting for his arrival.
The hero now crouches down on a mat and all the men squat
down round him in a circle. The old man goes up to him and
urinates over him from head to toe. If he is a good friend of the
hero he will deluge him with urine – this makes the honour shown
him all the greater (pp. 185–6).

As to the origin of this strange rite, the author informs
us that 'many rodents mark members of their pack to
identify them as belonging to the group'; and that the
urinating ceremony could be 'an analogous behaviour
pattern which in the course of time was transformed by other

* Reviewed in the *Sunday Times*, 18 February 1972.

79

races into rites in which water is used, such as baptism in
our own culture'.

Maybe. Could be. But why the analogy with rodents,
who are after all far removed from us, whereas no ethologist,
as far as I know, has reported similar goings-on among
our relatives, the primates? Or could it be that the fun-
loving Hottentots played a practical joke on the visitor
whom Professor Irenaus Eibl-Eibesfeldt quotes as his *only*
source of information relating to this alleged custom? The
visitor was a Herr P. Kolbe, and his book, *Gegenwärtiger
Zustand des Vorgebirges der Guten Hoffnung*, was published in
1719.

Contemporary ethologists have developed wonderful
techniques of observation for minute details of animal
behaviour. When it comes to human behaviour they have a
tendency to indulge in wild theorizings based on the flimsiest
evidence. Why do lovers kiss? Not because of what the
uninformed layman thinks, but because once upon a time
the young of our ancestors were fed mouth-to-mouth by
their mothers. 'This interpretation of kissing with lips and
tongue as ritualized feeding is supported by the fact that
lovers like exchanging delicacies while kissing . . .' (p. 133).
It could be objected that some people are given to kissing
parts of the body from which no food can be expected to
issue – the nape of the neck, for instance; but there is an
answer to that conundrum too. Chimpanzees practise the
'love bite' ('*Beisskuss*') applied with wide open mouth to
the partner's head. 'As this is the reply to a gesture of invitation to delousing one can interpret the love bite as a
ritualized grooming action. This interpretation finds support
in man from the fact that in giving a love bite one nibbles a
person's skin, and that in rare cases the teeth are still used
in skin grooming. I have filmed a Waika woman biting
impurities away from her husband's skin . . . Tongue-
flicking (*züngeln*) – like the love bite – must be derived
from an action of social grooming. On a Mediterranean
beach I filmed a girl who was patiently scratching away

and squeezing out small pimples for her male companion. Caressing and rubbing certainly belong in this complex of social grooming action as well ... By running their hands over their male partners' skin girls at once discover any small irregularities. In this sense caressing fulfils yet another task in the service of body care' (pp. 131, 141–2).

Could be. Maybe. It is quite amusing stuff as long as you do not take it too seriously. And the layman may derive comfort from the fact that ethologists do not take each other too seriously either. Desmond Morris in *The Naked Ape* startled us all with the theory that the human female's prominent bust and lips were visual stimuli, substituted by evolution for the monkey female's buttocks and labia at a time when our ancestors turned from back-to-front to front-to-front mating. But Eibl-Eibesfeldt won't have any of it: 'His [Morris's] theory that the lips are copies of the labia does not bear examination.' Lips evolved 'with the evolution of mouth-to-mouth feeding. This explains why both men and women have them' (p. 147).

Nor does Freud fare better. The Oedipus complex is a fable: 'Nothing of the kind has been proved ... We are certainly aware of a very strong and powerfully emotional bond with our children. But sexual feelings do not enter into it' (p. 159). That settles the controversy. Noah's daughters were merely engaged in social grooming activities.

Professor Eibl-Eibesfeldt was a pupil of Konrad Lorenz and is the Director of one of the departments in Lorenz's Institute in Seefelden. But he does not agree with the thesis put forward in Lorenz's essay *On Aggression*, according to which the bonds of affection among members of a social group are derived from ritualized forms of aggression. The main purpose of Eibl-Eibesfeldt's book is twofold: to refute the claim of the environmentalist school that all human behaviour is acquired by learning and restore innate instincts to their rightful place; and to show that this instinctual equipment is not confined to aggressive behaviour but also includes a disposition for friendship and co-operation – or love for short. To any reader who feels that these points need proving, the book may be recommended.

Hypnotic Horizons

Mind and Body by Stephen Black*

Chapter 2 of this book is called 'My Definition of Life'. Chapter 3 is called 'My Definition of Mind'. The first definition, set in italics, reads:

Life is a quality of matter which arises from the informational content inherent in the improbability of form.

The second definition, also in italics, sounds more cheerful:

Mind is the informational system derived from the sum improbability of form inherent in the material substance of living things.

Chapter 7 is called 'My Definition of a Psychosomatic Phenomenon.' It reads:

In my terms, the only criterion of a psychosomatic phenomenon will be taken as evidence of cure or symptomatic relief of a physical condition by psychotherapy.

What this last quotation means is that an illness is to be attributed to psychological causes if, and only if, it responds to psychological treatment. A debatable point, and one has to read that paragraph three times to get the meaning. The

* Reviewed in the *Observer*, 20 April 1969.

83

book is abominably written, with a disregard for grammar and syntax which makes some passages ambiguous, others incomprehensible; as a result, most readers, I fear, will be tempted to give up the struggle half-way through it. But that would be a great mistake, for Dr Black is a recognized authority on hypnotic research, and his brilliant experimental work, described in the concluding chapters of the book, has a direct bearing on the mind–body problem.

As a compromise, however, I would suggest that the reader skip the first 150 pages of Dr Black's muddled theorizings, further obscured by the fashionable jargon of information theory (see the first two 'definitions' quoted above). There is indeed a striking contrast between the originality of the author's research work and the naïveté of his philosophical ideas. Even his attempt to explain how hypnosis works ends in confusion. As far as one can make out, he regards it as a Pavlovian conditioned reflex, elicited by rhythmic stimulation and/or by the constriction of movement through swaddling in infancy, which 'continues to produce the conditional response of the relative immobility of foetal life. It is here that the catatonia accompanying animal hypnosis is so important.'

It is amusing to remember that, some years ago, Geoffrey Gorer came to exactly the opposite conclusions regarding the effects of swaddling on Russian babies: 'This inhibition of movement is felt to be extremely painful and frustrating and is responded to with intense destructive rage.'[1] Now Dr Black tells us that swaddling causes not rage, but hypnotic trance. Gorer relied on anthropological evidence; Black on the analogy between the swaddled baby and the catatonic state of the chicken forcibly laid on its back. Whatever the truth of the matter is, surely Black ought to have referred, at least in a footnote, to Gorer's opposite hypothesis.

The value of the book lies in the author's experimental work over the last ten years, previously published in the

British Medical Journal and learned periodicals, which is summarized in Chapters 11 to 14.

The uses of hypnosis in dentistry, obstetrics and in the treatment of skin diseases are by now generally known – if not generally accepted by the more conservative-minded in the profession. Dr Black himself is sensibly cautious in his clinical approach; he repeatedly points out that complete anaesthesia can only be induced in 'deep' hypnotic trance, and that only 5 per cent of the population are 'deep trance subjects' (about 35 per cent, according to his statistics, can be put into a medium trance and nearly everybody into a light trance). This puts a severe limitation on the direct therapeutic uses of hypnosis in clinical medicine: 'In the treatment of any condition by hypnosis, it is already a twenty-to-one chance that the result will be mostly negative.'

Nevertheless, on the privileged 5 per cent of deep-trance subjects all sorts of magic can be worked – from Esdaile's major operations carried out under hypnotic anaesthesia a century ago, to the disappearance of warts, birthmarks and nail deformities in response to hypnotic suggestion. Perhaps the most important breakthrough in this field was Albert Mason's now historic cure by hypnosis, in 1952, of a sixteen-year-old boy suffering from ichthyosis or fish-skin disease – a dreadful congenital affliction in which, owing to a functional deficiency of the skin glands, the patient's skin has the appearance of grey-green scales with an offensive smell. The condition was believed to be incurable. Mason, in a thoroughly controlled experiment, gave the boy a series of hypnotic treatments, concentrating his verbal suggestions first on one arm, then on the other, then on the legs and body, until, in a matter of weeks, the scales were replaced by normal skin. The publication of the cure in the *British Medical Journal* hit the headlines of the popular press, and though Mason was never able to cure another case of ichthyosis (presumably because the patients were not deep-trance subjects), a reviewer in the *British Medical Journal* rightly

85

commented that this single case was enough to require 'a revision of current concepts on the relation between mind and body'.

It was obviously with that kind of programme in mind that Black joined forces with Mason in their joint experiments on the suppression of allergic skin responses under hypnosis. The complex experimental design can only be summarized here in a simplified way. The pilot study was carried out on Mrs R., a middle-aged housewife, who, for the last twelve years, had suffered from incapacitating asthma and hay-fever during the 'pollen season', May to July. As traditional treatments had brought no relief, Mrs R. was sent by her doctor to Mason 'to try hypnosis'. Mason started with his weekly treatments about a month before the hay-fever season and, as a result, for the first time in twelve years Mrs R. remained completely free from any of the symptoms of asthma and hay-fever.

But that was not the point of the experiment. That relief of symptoms through hypnosis can be achieved in some cases of hay-fever and asthma was already known. What Black and Mason were after was not symptom-therapy, but to induce a more profound physiological change. Like most of her fellow sufferers, Mrs R. was allergic to the pollens of certain grasses, flowers and trees; when extracts of these allergens were injected into arm or leg, they produced the characteristic reactions of redness, swelling, heat, etc. During the first eight weeks of the treatment, when Mason's verbal suggestions referred exclusively to the suppression of the respiratory symptoms, the skin reactions, too, were partially abolished. In the ninth week, the specific suggestion was added that there should be no skin reaction to the pollen tests. The reaction vanished completely and with dramatic suddenness.

Black then repeated the experiment on a series of volunteers (selected from hundreds of candidates, as they had to be both allergic and capable of deep trance). Out of twelve subjects, eight responded to hypnotic suggestion with partial or total inhibition of the skin reaction; four failed to respond. Two thirds positive results were good enough by any standard; but how was it done? How could a hypnotic suggestion work such changes in fundamental processes on the level of cellular chemistry? Black was able to show that it was *not* done by changes in the blood flow, i.e., the contraction of capillaries in the test area, nor by the action of adrenal hormones – which would have been less baffling.

His subsequent experiments proved that the so-called Mantoux reaction could also be abolished by hypnosis. People who in their childhood had a harmless bout of tuberculosis become allergic to the Koch bacillus – which is why, before the advent of the antibiotics, a second infection was so often fatal. The allergy can be demonstrated by injection of the attenuated bacillus into the skin, where in 'Mantoux positive' individuals it causes swelling, redness, etc. But hypnosis can change a Mantoux positive into a Mantoux negative subject; and the physiological changes in the tissues of the test area, brought about by verbal suggestion, can actually be shown under the microscope.

The remaining two chapters describe experiments on hypnotically induced partial deafness – where perception of notes of a certain pitch is blocked out while hearing otherwise remains intact; and on the effect of hypnotically induced hallucinations on the subject's brain-waves, as recorded by the electroencephalograph. As far as the E.E.G. record is concerned, the effect of a hallucination seems to be indistinguishable from that of a 'real' experience.

As a therapeutic technique, hypnosis appears to be of only limited value; as a research tool to probe into the relations of mind and matter, it is invaluable. When we have gained an understanding of how a verbal command can change the reactivity of body tissues on a microscopic level, the world

The Heel of Achilles

will look different not only to the scientist, but also to the philosopher and theologian.

REFERENCE

1. *The People of Great Russia*, p. 123.

Anatomy of a Canard

Rumour in Orléans by Edgar Morin*

In May–June 1969, the staid city of Orléans, devoted to the cult of the Maid, was convulsed by a strange attack of mass hysteria. The most reliable account of the episode was published by *Le Monde* on 7 June of that year:

'Disappearance' of Women in Orléans: Plot or Hoax?

Scene: a women's dress shop on a main shopping street somewhere in the provinces, late one afternoon. A couple appears. The man decides to wait outside on the pavement while his wife goes into the boutique on her own. After a while the husband gets tired of waiting, goes into the establishment himself – and is informed that no person answering the description he gives has crossed the threshold of the shop. Confronted with this stubborn and obstructive attitude on the part of the staff, he goes to the police . . . The latter discover three women (including his wife) down in the basement, bound, gagged, chloroformed, ready to be shipped off abroad: a clear case of 'white slaving'.

This odd story is a complete fabrication. Yet though it is about as murkily fantastic as the plot of a bad thriller, it spread through the entire town in a matter of hours. Today it lies at the heart of every kind of fear and anxiety; it nurtures old resentments,

* Reviewed in the *Sunday Times*, 4 July 1971.

89

releases unacknowledged feelings of hatred, encourages folly and dissipates boredom. For nearly three weeks now Orléans has been living through a period of denunciation and calumny . . . Everyone suspects everyone else . . . headmistresses issue stern warnings to their girls, the 'suspect' shops are deserted, old scores are being paid off all round, and a collective psychosis of unparalleled dimensions is developing.

At the height of the rumour altogether twenty-six girls were said to have disappeared (all friends or cousins of one's best friend) although not a single case of a missing female had been reported to the police. All were said to have been drugged in the fitting-rooms of six fashionable boutiques, all six owned by Jews, and their inert bodies transported through a subterranean network of tunnels, sewers and catacombs to the Loire, where a submarine was waiting to carry them to a fate worse than death.

Why were none of the guilty shopkeepers arrested? Because the police were in the pay of the Jewish white-slavers. And so on; there is no need to go into details; they have an all-too-familiar ring. But there was no pogrom: the rumour collapsed as suddenly as it had come into being, partly under the sheer weight of its own absurdity, partly because various official and professional bodies, from the Prefecture to the Communist Party of the Loiret, took the counter-offensive when the situation got really ugly.

How did the story originate? Like other misfortunes that befell Orléans, it seems to have been engineered in England. In 1968 Heinemann published a book by Stephen Barley called *Sex Slavery*. It contained an item which in every detail (fashion boutique – suspicious husband – drugged wife in cellar) corresponded to the Orléans story, except that it was supposed to have happened in Grenoble and that there was no mention of Jews. A French translation of the book appeared in 1969; and on 6 May, just before the Orléans rumour started, the popular magazine *Noir et Blanc* reproduced that item without indication of its source, and giving the impression that it was reporting a recent event.

The Orléans police believe that it was this story which started the avalanche, during the week after the magazine reached the news-stands.

M. Morin is described on the blurb of his book as 'one of the directors of the Centre for the Study of Mass Communications at the Ecole Pratique des Hautes Etudes in Paris'. He also appears to be the founder of a school which he alternatively refers to as 'clinical sociology', 'occurential sociology' and '*sociologie du présent*'. In July 1969, one month after the event, he descended on Orléans with a team of five young collaborators (two of them 'with long hair and hippie necklaces') to carry out, *in three days* (p. 14), a field study of the history and social implications of the rumour. His book adds no new facts to the reports published by the French press, and leaves us no wiser regarding the 'unexplored depth of the collective subconscious' which it was meant to elucidate. The unexplored depths seem to consist either of tautologies – 'from the very outset, the modernization of this erotic myth was in fact no more than the crystallization of a modern myth with erotic overtones' (p. 76) – or else clichés, archetypal chestnuts such as the Jew as a perennial scapegoat, adolescent fantasies of rape, old crones don't like miniskirts. These clichés are dressed up in a jargon both pretentious and obscure, which seems to enjoy a great vogue among contemporary French anthropologists. The last paragraph of M. Morin's book, under the headline 'Conclusion', may serve as a conclusive example:

Thus we take up a position at the dialectical mid-point between event and theory, history and sociology, the contemporary and the anthropological, and – more specifically in this case – between phenomenon and discipline, crisis and system, the actual and the potential, trend and counter-trend, evolution and involution, the innovating and the archaic.

Could it be that the proverbial Cartesian Lucidity of the Gallic Spirit is also a myth – a Rumour in Orléans?

The Abishag Complex

The Greening of America by Charles A. Reich*

'*Pink*, v.i. (of a motor-engine) emit series of high-pitched explosive sounds caused by detonation of mixture following partial combustion.' I am not sure that Uncle Sam is greening, but he is certainly pinking, as defined above by the *Concise Oxford Dictionary*. Mr Reich uses even stronger language in the opening sentences of his book: 'America is dealing death, not only to people in other lands, but to its own people. So say the most thoughtful and passionate of our youth, from California to Connecticut.' However, he tells us, there is no reason for despair, because this same passionate youth is inspiring the nation with a new form of consciousness 'like flowers pushing up through the concrete pavement . . . a veritable greening of America'.

This new form of consciousness he calls 'Consciousness III'. The first eight of the twelve chapters of the book describe the bankruptcy of the two previous forms. 'Consciousness I' viewed America 'as if it were a world of small towns and simple virtues'. 'Consciousness II' was engendered by the technological revolution and the rise of what Mr Reich calls the 'Corporate State'. This is a thoroughly misleading

* Reviewed in the *Sunday Times*, 2 May 1971.

term, normally applied to the constitution which Mussolini, in 1926, imposed on Italy; its *Corporazioni sindicati fascisti* had hardly more in common with the structure of American society than Pigs have with pigs. Mr Reich's terminology becomes even more bewildering when we read (p. 247) that 'the liberal welfare state – [is] what we have called the Corporate State'.

What he means by his 'Consciousness II' are certain mental attitudes prevalent in contemporary American society: conformism and competitiveness; status-seeking; subjection to the mass media; and the related phenomena of alienation, pollution, wire-tapping, rat-racing – the whole menu. On all this one would willingly go along with him if it had not all been said before, and said more incisively, without Reich's exaggerations and distortions. To quote only one example: he compares the great global conflicts of our time to the artificial needs created by advertising:

> The 'need' for the Cold War and the Vietnam War has been created like the 'need' for that other characteristic product of the Corporate State, a new high-powered car ... The threat from a primitive people ten thousand miles away is imaginary ... an intellectual creation, a 'new product.'

On this view of history, the rape of Czechoslovakia in 1948, which started the Cold War, was a figment of the imagination of 'Consciousness II'. To discuss, as Reich does, the mental state of a great power out of its international context, without any reference to the pressures acting on it, leads to absurdity.

One wonders how it came about that such a muddle-headed book has been at the top of the American bestseller list for several months. The answer lies in the concluding chapters on 'Consciousness III', which promises a cure for all the evils of modern society, and the realization of Utopia – without bloodshed, class war or even political upheaval:

> There is revolution coming. It will not be like revolutions of the past. It will originate with the individual and with culture, and it

93

will change the political structure only as its final act. It will not require violence to succeed, and it cannot be successfully resisted by violence . . . It will be 'revolution by consciousness'.

How one longs to believe Mr Reich. And how avidly one scans his book for the recipe, the magic formula, which will lead us from our air-conditioned desert into the Promised Land. The leaders, as already indicated, are the young:

> This is the revolution of the new generation. Their protest and rebellion, their culture, clothes, music, drugs, ways of thought and liberated life-style are not a passing fad or a form of dissent and refusal, nor are they in any sense irrational. The whole emerging pattern, from ideals to campus demonstrations to beads and bell-bottoms to the Woodstock festival, makes sense and is part of a consistent philosophy. It is both necessary and inevitable, and in time it will include not only youth, but all people in America.

The young have achieved their liberating revolutionary consciousness by finding a model to emulate: 'It was the hip–black life-style, with its contempt for the white middle-class values and its affirmation of the sensual, the earthy and the rebellious elements in man, that gave high-school and college students something to copy instead of the existing pattern.'

Mr Reich's admiration for young people copying the hip–black life-style is touchingly uncritical. He denies that they are 'irrational' although they make a point of affirming it; he ascribes to them a 'consistent philosophy' which is the first thing they reject. They have 'the energy of enthusiasm, of happiness, of hope . . . other generations never had such energy even in their youth' (p. 172). Their 'clothes are earthy and sensual. They express an affinity with nature . . . They don't show dirt, they are good for lying on the ground . . .' (p. 173. 'Members of the new generation seek out the beach, the woods and the mountains. They do not litter these places with beer cans, they do not shatter the silences with power boats or motorcycle noises' (p. 193). Perhaps Mr Reich is hard of hearing.

94

Their intellectual powers verge on clairvoyance: 'The Consciousness III person, no matter how young and in-experienced he may be, seems to possess an extraordinary "new knowledge" . . .' He 'sees effortlessly what is phony or dishonest in politics . . . whereas an older person has to go through years of education to make himself equally aware . . . Nothing is more difficult for an older person to believe in than this "new knowledge", but it is such a striking phenomenon, extending even to long-haired California teenagers hitchhiking their way to the beach, whose experi-ence with political thinking or newspaper reading is limited' (pp. 192–3). Mr Reich nowhere explains why so many of his intellectual prodigies regard Mao's Thoughts as the new gospel.

It is becoming increasingly difficult for the not-so-young to look at the young with neither a jaundiced nor a moist eye. Those who take the latter attitude seem to suffer from a psychological affliction which one might call the Abishag Complex . . . 'Now King David was old and stricken in years; and they covered him with clothes, but he gat no heat.' So they put in his bed a beautiful young virgin, Abishag the Shunammite, and he 'lay in her bosom' to warm his old bones, but that was all that happened. Never has the Abishag Complex been so rampant as among faculty mem-bers of American universities at the dawn of 'Consciousness III'. Mr Reich, unlike Professor Marcuse, is only forty-three, but he teaches law at a university where the 'cut-off point for being trusted' is thirty.

However, he concedes that even the thirty-plus generation can participate in the revolution by consciousness and attain liberation, if they are willing to learn from the young and to change their life-style and goals: 'The employee liberates himself by turning his back on the institutional goals of advancement in the hierarchy, status and security' (p. 225). It is as simple as that. The member of a business organization 'should take the position, in his official capacity, that further growth of his organization is undesirable' because money for hospitals is more important (p. 234). Generally speaking, the underlying principle of 'Consciousness III' 'is a non-material set of values. For older people, 'a new consciousness could rest on growing a garden, reading literature, baking bread, playing Bach on a recorder, or developing a new sense of family, so long as it represents a true knowledge of self, rather than false consciousness' (p. 205).

True enough – but hardly shattering news. Who has said all this before – John Bunyan or Abraham Lincoln? Or was it Voltaire who declared that the end of all wisdom was to cultivate one's garden – I mean, doing one's thing?

In the meantime the pinking of the great power engine continues, less audible at times, but no less disquieting. Less optimistic than Mr Reich, I feel that the greening is not yet in view.

Prophet and Poseur

Antimemoirs by André Malraux, translated
by Terence Kilmartin*

In an autobiographical book, years ago, I described my first
meeting with Malraux. In 1934 I was honorary treasurer of
an anti-Nazi set-up in Paris called I.N.F.A. (Institut pour
l'Etude du Fascisme) and was making the rounds of French
intellectuals, asking them for donations:

It was in this capacity that I first met André Malraux. I went
to see him at his office at Gallimard's, the publishers, and we
talked while walking up and down in the garden at the back of
the Gallimard building. As a fervent admirer of Malraux's, I was
overwhelmed by the occasion, but went on bravely about the
great prospects of I.N.F.A. and its even greater need for donations.
Malraux listened in silence, occasionally uttering one of his
characteristic, awe-inspiring nervous sniffs, which sounded like
the cry of a wounded jungle beast and were followed by a slap of
his palm against his nose. At first this was rather startling, but
one soon got accustomed to it. When I had had my say, Malraux
stopped, advanced towards me threateningly, until I had my back
against the garden wall, and said:
'*Oui, oui, mon cher, mais que pensez-vous de l'apocalypse?*'

* Reviewed in the *Observer*, 22 September 1968.

With that he gave me five hundred francs, and wished me good luck.

Although later on we met frequently and were on friendly terms, that phrase and gesture sticks out of the past like the Eiffel Tower – a moving and faintly absurd landmark. It was the essential Malraux, genuinely obsessed with the *nostalgie de l'apocalypse* and yet giving the impression that he was play-acting *pour épater*. At the very beginning of his *Antimemoirs*, he speaks of 'an intellectual problem which interested me a great deal: how to reduce to the minimum the play-acting side of one's nature'. He may have sincerely tried, but he was never successful in that particular endeavour: one cannot be a modern buccaneer, a hero of two wars, a dazzling orator, diplomatic envoy and a Cabinet Minister without a touch of showmanship in one's nature.

Yet in Malraux the dualism of prophet and *poseur* is more conspicuous than in other great adventurers that come to mind – more extreme even than in Malraux's own hero, T. E. Lawrence. It affects not only the man of action and public figure – which is unavoidable; it has also begun to pervade his writing – which is harder to accept. Lawrence, the public figure, may have been both prophet and *poseur*; Lawrence, the writer, succeeded in preserving his integrity (and so did St-Exupéry, Ignazio Silone, young Richard Hillary). But unhappily in Malraux's case the virus has begun to invade the tissue of his writing. The symptoms are page-long purple patches, punctuated by flourishes and passages of deliberate obscurity, pseudo-profundities and inflated emotions, which at times read as if they had been inspired by an overdose of L.S.D. Although a confirmed Malraux addict, I found entire chapters almost unreadable, a strain on the eyes desperately trying to discern the emperor's clothes.

Thus on the very first page of the book we are told: 'To reflect upon life – life in relation to death – is perhaps no more than to intensify one's questioning.' Surely this must mean something, but what? And this kind of thing is to be found on practically every page. Take this oracular dictum, attributed to Alain: 'When all's said and done, it is the purest and best in man which rules through reverence and admiration – and it has never existed' (the French original is even more obscure).

Another recurrent mannerism is his habit of making dark allusions to exotic events, obscure artists, archaeological curiosities and anthropological titbits unknown to ordinary mortals; a kind of esoteric name-dropping (one wonders why we are offered no quotations in Sanskrit and Mandarin). Traces of this vice could already be found in the *Musée Imaginaire* and the other art books; but now it has got worse. It creeps into most of the encounters and dialogues – with de Gaulle, Nehru, ambassadors, and statesmen; they are related in the same style of compulsive obliquity, of secrets shared by the cognoscenti. Through entire chapters we seem to move in a world of Nietzschean supermen, talking in divine riddles; while all basic information about the countries and personalities is tantalisingly withheld.

Thus we learn nothing about French politics during the post-war years, nothing about the fundamental state of affairs in India or China during the author's visits, and nothing, except a few dramatic highlights, about the author's life. He says: 'I have called this book *Antimemoirs* because it answers a question which memoirs do not pose, and does not answer those which they do.' With the second half of this sentence one must agree, but the answer mentioned in the first half I failed to discover. What, then, is the book about?

It is, in fact, neither an auto- nor an anti-biography, but a conglomeration of chapters from previous novels and episodic reports of recent and earlier travels and encounters. They are stitched together, with deliberate disregard for chronological or thematic order, by threads of associations which are no doubt relevant to the author, but not always to the reader. Thus, considered as a whole, and in view of the high expectations raised by the oblique promise of the title, the book is a disappointment. But if one regards it simply as an omnibus collection of independent pieces, the picture changes altogether. While some of these pieces may be unreadable, for the reasons I have tried to indicate, and can safely be skipped, there are others representative of the best writing of one of the best writers of our time.

We meet again several of the familiar masterpieces: the madcap expedition with Corniglion-Molinier in a single-engined plane to the ruins of the alleged city of the Queen of Sheba; the fight with the hurricane over Tunis; the struggle to get the trapped tank going (the most Kafkaesque war episode I know – the trapped giant tank becomes an allegory of the helpless beetle in 'Metamorphosis', which becomes an allegory of the helplessness of man).

In these action stories, where the adversary is never a human being but death itself in various guises, while the hero's reactions oscillate between horror and sexual excitement, Malraux shows what a superb reporter he is, and how fluid the boundaries are between 'literature' and 'reportage'. This applies equally to the great action chapters in his earlier novels and to the all-too-few newly written episodes in the book – such as facing a murderously hostile audience in Guyana and facing the Gestapo as a captured Maquis leader. In these passages, the man of action and the man of letters coalesce into a monolithic unit; the results are masterpieces. And so are some of his public speeches – such as the unforgettable funeral oration for the murdered Resistance leader, Jean Moulin; one marvelled at the perfect harmony between the author who improvised the script and the actor who delivered it. But in his electoral speeches, when the actor got the upper hand over the author, the result was often a kind of purple waffle, delivered to the accompaniment of a *fanfare obscure*. And the same applies whenever the comedian invades the writer's study – which brings us back to my starting-point.

The only wisdom I acquired when I travelled through Asia in search of Yogis and Zen Masters was a lesson childishly simple once one had learnt it: never ask yourself whether a 'holy man' is a saint or a phoney, but try to draw a balance-sheet of the amounts of saintliness and phoneyness in him. *Mutatis mutandis*: even the worst chapters in this book amount to no more than a temporary deficit on the balance-sheet of the author of *La Condition humaine*; the man who created the Spanish International Air Force during the Civil War; who was one of the most effective leaders of the French Resistance; who cleaned historic Paris from centuries of grime, and had the ceiling of the Opéra painted by Chagall.

If we had a few Malrauxs in this country, intellectuals would perhaps be treated less condescendingly.

Telepathy and Dialectics

Psychic Discoveries by the Russians, edited by Martin Ebon*

In the course of the last decade, garbled accounts in the Western press told of a curious vogue in parapsychology in the Soviet Union. The names of two female prodigies, Rosa Kuleschova and Ninel Kulagina, kept cropping up: Rosa was allegedly able to read, blindfolded, with her fingertips, while Ninel was reported (and filmed) moving about light objects such as cigarettes and matches lying on a table, without touching them, by telekinesis – i.e., a sheer effort of will. Rosa was occasionally caught peeping from under her blindfold, while Ninel (originally called Nelya; she changed her name to Lenin spelt backwards) was reported to have been convicted for fraud, unconnected with her psychic activities. But that is neither here nor there. Both Rosa and Nelya had been submitted to controlled tests by Soviet scientists in high academic positions, who testified that the phenomena they produced were genuine. But that again is neither there nor elsewhere. Occasional cheating on a bad day does not prove or disprove anything – even austere chemistry teachers were known to 'cook' their experiments when something went wrong. On the other hand, one wonders how strict the con-

* Reviewed in the *New Statesman*, 4 May 1973.

trols of the 'controlled' tests have been, and whether they would have stood up to the wiles of a clever stage magician. Thus, even if one's personal attitude towards parapsychology is a positive one, the wisest course to adopt in such cases is expressed by the maxim of an eminent Moscow physicist: 'When I hear the doorbell of my apartment, I am inclined to assume that it is the postman ringing, and not the Queen of England.'

However, these two sensational ladies, and their host of imitators, are merely the fringe phenomena of respectable, academic E.S.P. research in the Soviet Union. Another phenomenon is 'the magnificent Messing' – the star of stage hypnotists and thought-readers, said to have been a personal protégé of Stalin. It is rather a pity that Martin Ebon has seen fit to include an uncritically admiring article about this mountebank in his informative anthology. The article is written by a Polish journalist and based on Messing's autobiography – where he relates that in 1915 he met Freud and Einstein in Vienna: 'Freud was, apparently, so intrigued by Messing's faculties that he invited him to his own place where Messing gave a performance, in Einstein's presence – Freud himself acting as inductor for several complicated experiments, all with positive results.'

There is no record of Einstein having visited Vienna in 1915, nor of a meeting with Freud, and the whole episode is patently absurd. Yet Messing's spurious autobiography was serialized in the Soviet periodical *Science and Religion* (designed for anti-religious propaganda) and this fact alone is characteristic of the new party line towards parapsychology – which could be described as periodically wavering between benevolence, ambivalence and an occasional mildly hostile blast from *Pravda*.

There are several threads interwoven in this confused scene. Some strategists of the ideological front may feel that permissiveness towards 'occult superstitions' may provide a relatively harmless outlet for repressed religious cravings – better a Lenin spelt backwards than a new Rasputin. But there seems to be another reason for increasing official support for serious research into telepathy, which is of a rather fantastic nature. In 1959, the French boulevard press published reports, which were taken up by the more serious journal *Science et Vie*, to the effect that the American nuclear submarine *Nautilus* had been in telepathic communication with its home base while it was submerged under the polar ice. Odd as it may seem, one of the key people who believed in this report was Professor Leonid L. Vassiliev, Head of the Psychology Department at Leningrad University and bearer of the Order of Lenin. Vassiliev himself had for some twenty-five years carried out telepathic experiments in his department, but had kept the matter rather quiet. The *Nautilus* reports convinced him – and others – that the time was ripe for action. 'E.S.P. – extra-sensory perception,' he declared at a meeting of scientists, 'could be of gigantic significance for science and life, should the hypothesis based on our experiments prove correct; namely, that telepathic transmission is accomplished by some kind of energy or factor so far unknown to us . . . To discover such energy or factor would be tantamount to the discovery of nuclear energy.' He published in quick succession two books setting out the results of the previously unknown parapsychological research work at his department, enlisted the support of such eminent academicians as Nikolai Semenov, Nobel laureate in chemistry and Vice-President of the Academy of Science, W. Tugerinov, Dean of the Philosophical Faculty in Leningrad, and, presumably, some influential people in military intelligence. Within a year, the first official parapsychology department was established at Leningrad University; others, at Moscow and elsewhere, followed. From 1960 onward, parapsychology in the Soviet Union had attained academic respectability and official support – though there was of course no lack of hostile critics. Similar developments have been reported from Czechoslovakia and Bulgaria.

In fact, however, parapsychology had merely broken the surface – like a submarine – for it had always existed in

Russia, before and after the Revolution. Pavlov's successor, Vladimir Bekhterev, Head of the Institute for Brain Research in Leningrad, experimented in the early 1920s with two telepathic dogs, belonging to the celebrated circus performer, Durov, and published papers attesting the genuineness of the phenomena; Durov was subsequently put in charge of a specially created Zoo-Psychological Laboratory in Moscow, which was closed down at his death in 1934. But interest in animal telepathy continued. One recent Russian experiment, both ingenious and ghastly, was described by Professor Naumov at the Moscow Conference on Technological Parapsychology in June 1968. A litter of young rabbits was placed in a submarine. The mother remained in the laboratory, wired to an electroencephalograph which recorded its brain-waves. At prearranged times the young rabbits on the submerged vessel were killed one after the other. According to the report, the E.E.G. record showed a violent disturbance of the mother rabbit's brain-activity at the exact moment of each killing. No further details of the experiment are available; rumour has it that they are classified. But one thing is obvious: you can't take a litter of rabbits on a military submarine without official permission.

Naïve Westerners may wonder how all this benevolence toward the occult can be reconciled with Marxist–Leninist dialectical materialism. Much more easily, it seems, than one would have imagined. For one thing, the obnoxious terms 'parapsychology' and 'psychical research' are replaced by respectable euphemisms such as 'bio-information', 'biological communication' and 'psychotronics'. Next, you turn the table on your opponents, as Professor Vassiliev did, when he wrote that psychical research could have a 'strictly materialistic basis and serve to counteract superstitious interpretations'. The psychiatrist A. Roshchin supported him in a public debate by arguing that if materialistic science turns its back on telepathy 'this will doubtless be the open door through which religious faith rushes in'. I shall not be surprised if we soon hear some worthy Soviet academician proclaim that to deny the immortality of the soul is an unscientific attitude which plays into the hands of religious superstition.

Psychic Discoveries by the Russians is a valuable source of information on a significant ideological development in Russia which to most Westerners will come as a surprise.

Wittgensteinomania

Wittgenstein's Vienna by Allan Janik and Stephen Toulmin*

When he had completed his *Tractatus Logico-Philosophicus*, Ludwig Wittgenstein wrote a letter to his friend Professor Ficker which gave a new twist to the parable of the emperor's clothes (the italics are Wittgenstein's):

> *The book's point is an ethical one.* I once meant to include in the preface a sentence which is not in fact there now, but which I will write out for you here, because it will perhaps be a key to the work for you. What I meant to write, then, was this. My work consists of two parts: the one presented here plus all that I have *not* written. And *it is precisely this second part that is the important one* . . . I believe that where *many* others today are just *gassing*, I have managed in my book to put everything firmly into place by being silent about it.

The *Tractatus* became one of the most influential philosophical works of our century, the source of an esoteric cult, the dark oracle from which such diverse schools as Logical Positivism, the Vienna Circle and the Linguistic Philosophers of Oxford drew their inspiration. But unavoidably – as naïve non-philosophers would expect – their interpretations of Wittgenstein's message were based on what he had written,

* Reviewed in the *Observer*, 3 June 1973.

and not on that second part which he had *not* written. And as far as the written text goes, the message could be summed up in a simple slogan: 'Metaphysicians shut your trap.' Proposition 6.53 – the last but second – in the *Tractatus* reads (my italics):

The right method of philosophy would be this. To say nothing except what can be said, i.e. the propositions of natural science, i.e. something *that has nothing to do with philosophy*: and then always, when someone else wished to say something metaphysical, to demonstrate to him that he had given no meaning to certain signs in his propositions.

The disciples followed this prescription to the letter. All problems which the layman thought to be the basic pre-occupation of philosophers – ethical values, moral judgements, free will and determinism, the nature of consciousness and the meaning of life – were confined as meaningless to the rubbish heap. The result, as Ernest Gellner remarked, was 'an inverted vision which treats genuine thought as a disease'. Bertrand Russell, who had written an enthusiastic Introduction to Wittgenstein's *Tractatus*, thirty years later wrote an equally enthusiastic Introduction to Gellner's *Words and Things* which could be called an *Anti-Tractatus*: 'The later Wittgenstein,' Russell wrote, 'seems to have grown tired of serious thinking and to have invented a doctrine which would make such an activity unnecessary.'

Wittgenstein himself maintained that everybody had mis-understood him, starting with Russell himself (whose Preface he initially rejected as misleading); he repudiated the Oxford Linguists, the Vienna Circle and the Logical Positivists ('the trouble with Ayer is, he's clever *all* the time'). Thus, apparently, these dominant schools of philosophy – or anti-philosophy – of the middle of our century were founded on a monstrous misunderstanding of the message of its principal prophet.

This, at least, is the contention of the authors of the present book. They also maintain that the main influence on

Wittgenstein's intellectual formation was not the Cambridge of Russell and Moore (as is generally believed) but Vienna during the decline of the Habsburg Empire. Their 'central hypothesis about Viennese culture' is 'that to be a *fin-de-siècle* Viennese artist or intellectual . . . one had to face the problem of *the nature and limits of language, expression and communication*' (their italics). Confronted with this task, young Wittgenstein set out to explore the frontiers of language, logic and reason and to stake out their boundaries. When he got to Cambridge at the age of twenty-two, Russell and Moore provided him with the technical tools of his undertaking. The upshot of his labours was that language is an excellent means of representation and communication as far as the world of facts is concerned, but cannot cope adequately with the ultimates of experience – emotions, aesthetic values, ethical intuitions. *Sätze können nichts Höheres ausdrücken*' (6.42) – 'Sentences cannot express anything pertaining to the higher realms . . . It is clear that ethics cannot be expressed' (6.421). And as a climax, the celebrated last proposition (which also appears in the Preface) : 'Whereof one cannot speak, thereof one must be silent.'

One might call it a winged tautology. (Gertrude Stein is remembered by her rose ; God explained to Moses 'I am that I am'.) The misunderstanding of the message arose, it seems, because Wittgenstein took that phrase literally : what really mattered to him – the *Höheres*, the ultimate – thereof he remained silent. Hence the remark that the important part of the book is the one that he did *not* write – and the pathetic assertion that 'the book's point is an ethical one'. If so, the reader could not help missing it, since the point was made in invisible ink. The visible part represented a brilliant demolition job, reducing metaphysics to meaninglessness, reason to ethical neutrality, philosophy to a proudly proclaimed impotence.

More than a century before Wittgenstein, Schopenhauer had written: 'To preach morality is hard ; to give it an intellectual justification is impossible.' Rarely has the human predicament been summed up in a more concise formula. The *Tractatus* provides modern variations on this theme in a more sophisticated vein, orchestrated by the symbolic logic of Frege and Russell; whether it added something of value remains an open question. But there can be little doubt that its author was a mouthpiece of the *Zeitgeist*, producing astonishing resonance effects. 'Philosophers who never met him,' wrote Gilbert Ryle in 1951, the year of Wittgenstein's death, 'can be heard talking philosophy in his tone of voice; and students who can barely spell his name now wrinkle up their noses at things which had a bad smell for him.'

The profound impact he made on Cambridge seems to have been partly due to his gift of beating the dons at their own game of eccentric behaviour, odd-ballship and cussedness. He countered their understatements with the preposterous boast in the Preface to the *Tractatus* that 'the *truth* of the thoughts' contained in it was 'unassailable and definitive'; and that thereby the problems of philosophy 'have in essentials been finally solved'. His modesty was equally provocative: when he became a fellow of Trinity College, he refused to dine at High Table because it stood on a platform six inches higher than the main floor; he had to be served at a separate card-table set up on floor-level. Combined with this exhibitionism there was a masochistic streak: he spent long periods in menial occupations – as a hospital orderly in the Second World War, and as a teacher in elementary schools in small Austrian villages. There was also a pathological streak: *three* of Wittgenstein's four brothers committed suicide; and Wittgenstein himself complained in his letters of his own 'rottenness', obviously connected with problems of sex.

But these traits in Wittgenstein's personality, which could not have been without influence on his philosophy, are only mentioned by the authors in passing. Nevertheless, their book provides an original, and highly controversial, interpretation of one of the oddest episodes in the history of philosophy – a man setting out to circumcise logic and all but succeeding in castrating thought.

In Memory of A. D. Peters

The end of this section dealing with books is perhaps the appropriate place for the following obituary note on my late friend and literary agent, A. D. Peters.*

Some literary agents act as nannies to their authors; others as promoters or procurers; A. D. Peters, who died on 3 February 1973, at the age of eighty, was clearly predestined to become a revered father-figure to successive generations of writers, regardless of their age and sex.

He was easy to like, difficult to know. His shyness and excessive reserve made him appear like a personage out of *The Forsythe Saga*; only his close friends knew the adventurous romantic inside the armour. Even his first names behind the coy' A. D.' were unknown to most. Intimates called him 'Peter'.

His origins were also known to only a few: he did not keep them a secret, but he never talked about them. At the age of eighty, he wrote a brief autobiographical sketch, the opening paragraphs of which read:

I, August Detlev, was born in Schleswig-Holstein, the fourth of seven children. My father was born a Dane, but thanks to Prussia acquiring the Kiel Canal, I was born German. Both descriptions

* Published in the *Sunday Times*, 4 February 1973.

III

are ethnologically wrong. Nearer the truth are the robbers and murderers who invaded East Anglia and founded the Anglo-Saxon race.

When I was three my father, a farmer, went bankrupt and four aunts took charge of his children . . . The aunt who adopted me ran a girls' school in Brighton, so I began life again a stranger in a strange land and the only boy in a girls' school, until I learnt English and some degree of civilization . . .

He went to Haberdashers' Aske's School in Hampstead, then to Cambridge, where in three years he got two degrees: in economics and modern languages.

In 1914 I spent July fooling around and deciding what to do. Very suddenly the war broke out. Off with two friends to join the Artists Rifles, get a commission and reach France before Christmas when the fun would have ended. But things went wrong. Born in Schleswig-Holstein! What does that make you? German. Enemy alien. Over to the secular arm. The police were remarkably kind considering that everyone else had gone mad and even a dachshund was not safe out-of-doors.

Eventually he got a job, keeping accounts in a slate mine in North Wales. In the summer of 1916 aliens were permitted to enlist – but only in a Labour Battalion, in which he served till 1919. (By a cruel irony, his only son, Richard, became a commando in the Second World War and was killed in Burma.)

In 1919 Peter landed his first job – as assistant editor of *The World*. Shortly he was made editor of this and other magazines published by Odhams. In 1923 he became bored with being an editor and infatuated with the stage. James Agate told him that the *Daily Chronicle* were looking for a new dramatic critic. He got that job too. A year later he gave it up – 'bored, disillusioned, no future'. By then, at the age of thirty-two, he had discovered his true vocation – neither an obvious nor an easy one. In May 1924 he started his literary agency. He realized – or imagined – that he did not have the makings of a first-class writer. This kind of insight turns many a bitter young man into a jaundiced literary critic; on Peter it had the opposite effect: he gave up his job as a critic and became a catalyst. If he could not write, he could help others to make a living by writing.

To be a literary catalyst requires a rare combination of gifts: absence of envy, affection for and patience with writers, discernment and sensitivity combined with a certain robustness in dealings with publishers, editors and other fiends. Peter had it all at his fingertips, as the agency's rise to prominence showed. In the early years he was joined by W. M. Roughhead and Margaret Stephens who became pillars of the firm. Among its earliest clients were Hilaire Belloc, Rebecca West, J. B. Priestley, Evelyn Waugh, Terence Rattigan and Cecil Day Lewis. The list kept expanding over nearly half a century, but was never allowed to exceed a critical limit, where personal contact would be lost.

There was another side to Peter's character about which few among his friends knew. He was an undercover philanthropist, a secret but passionate do-gooder, who helped in an unobtrusive way by donating time and money to various causes – such as the abolition of the death penalty, a fundraising campaign for refugee writers, and an annual competition for prisoners with awards for creative work in literature and the arts. In this last enterprise he acted for seven years as chairman of the board of trustees, fought against red tape in prison administration, did a large amount of reading and judging prisoners' literary entries – over three hundred a year – and became quite a familiar figure in Pentonville.

I am not alone among his authors who feel that A. D. Peters has conferred upon the profession of literary agent an aura of integrity, humanity and dignity which it had not possessed before.

H

'Nothing But . . . '?

Literature and the Law of Diminishing Returns*

In Solzhenitsyn's novel *The First Circle* some people are discussing scientific progress. Suddenly one of them, Gleb Nerzhin, bursts out:

Progress! Who wants progress? That's just what I like about art – the fact that there can't be any 'progress' in it. For example – in the seventeenth century there was Rembrandt, and nobody can improve on him, whereas seventeenth-century technology now looks very crude to us ...

He then talks about the tremendous advances in engineering since the 1870s, and reflects: 'But has there been any advance on *Anna Karenina*, which was written at that time?'

The opposite attitude was taken by Sartre in his essay 'What is Literature?', where he compared books with bananas which one can enjoy only while they are fresh. *Anna Karenina*, on this view, must have rotted long ago. The same attitude is expressed in a more provocative manner by spokesmen of the *nouveau roman* and other *avant-garde* groups, including some of the more articulate student-rebels. It is summed up in an epigrammatic statement by Antonin

* The Cheltenham Lecture, given at the Cheltenham Festival of Literature, November 1969.

Arteaud: 'The masterpieces of the past are for the past; they are not for us.'

Solzhenitsyn's hero reflects the conventional view that science progresses in a cumulative manner, brick upon brick, the way a tower is built, whereas art is timeless, a dance of coloured balls on the jets of a fountain, playing variations on a few eternal themes. If you accept this view, then it is pointless to search for any objective criteria of 'progress' in poetry, painting or drama; art, then, does not evolve, it merely formulates and reformulates the same archetypal experience in the idiom of the period; and though the vocabulary is subject to changes – including the optical vocabulary of the painter – the statement contained in a great work of art remains valid and unmarked by time's arrow.

The opposite view – that works of the past were good for the past, but are not good enough for the present – implies that art *does* progress and evolve. One cannot simply reject Tolstoy or Rembrandt or Etruscan painting on the relativistic grounds that they speak in an idiom *different* from ours; rejection implies the belief that we have discovered forms of expression that are *more pertinent* and valid than those of the past. Some spokesmen of the *avant-garde* of our time, and of the *avant-gardes* of past times, have in fact asserted at the top of their voices that they were the torch-bearers of objective progress in art – Impressionists, Expressionists, Abstractionists; and there is hardly a writer, past or present, who did not or does not believe in his heart of hearts his style and technique of writing to be closer to reality, both intellectually and emotionally, than those of the past. Let us face it: our reverence for Homer or Goethe is sweetened by a touch of condescension not unlike our attitude to infant prodigies: how clever they were for their age! how almost modern!

The belief that the art forms of the present are superior, or at least in some respects superior, to those of the past can be carried to grotesque extremes. For example, the *Guardian* published some time ago an article on 'Universities of the Future' which summarized the attitude of the rebellious students as follows:

The university is there to study the future ... Who needs the odes of Horace, of Marvell, of Keats? The absolute effective model of beat poetry or guitar poetry has made their pretended virtues only too relative.

But leaving such extremes aside, one's sympathies are unavoidably divided – or rather, they alternate – between the two camps: between the Gleb Nerzhins who hold that art is untouched by the vulgar march of progress, and those others who consider art as a kind of Olympic Games, where, thanks to improved techniques, athletes every four years produce new records. (Remember Hemingway boasting that he was still the champ.) As usual in such controversies, one suspects that both parties are guilty of bath-waterism – throwing away the opponent's baby with the bath.

Let me side-step for a moment from literature to the visual arts. This is an old gambit already used by Quintilian in the first century. To explain the development of Latin oratory from its erstwhile austerity to its flowery 'modern' style, Quintilian compared it to the progress of Greek sculpture from archaic rigidity to the smoothness and grace of the fourth century B.C. I am going to use a similar trick, and quote my favourite art historian, E. H. Gombrich, in support of the view that there *can* be cumulative progress in art, as there is in science:

In antiquity the discussion of painting and sculpture inevitably centred on [the] imitation [of nature] – mimesis. Indeed it may be said that the progress of art towards that goal was to the ancient what the progress of technology is to the modern: the model of progress as such. Thus Pliny told the history of sculpture and painting as the history of inventions, assigning definite achievements in the rendering of nature to individual artists: the painter Polygnotus was the first to represent people with open mouth and with teeth, the sculptor Pythagoras was the first to render nerves and veins, the painter Nikias was concerned with light and shade.

The history of these years [550 to 350 B.C.] as it is reflected in Pliny or Quintilian was handed down like an epic of conquest, a story of inventions . . . In the Renaissance it was Vasari who applied this technique to the history of the arts of Italy from the thirteenth to the sixteenth century. Vasari never fails to pay tribute to those artists of the past who made a distinct contribution, as he saw it, to the mastery of representation. 'Art rose from humble beginnings to the summit of perfection' [Vasari says] because such natural geniuses as Giotto blazed the trail and others were thus enabled to build on their achievements.[1]

Here, it seems, is the historic refutation of Nerzhin's thesis of the timelessness of art. 'If I could see further than others,' said Newton, 'it is because I stood on the shoulders of giants.' Leonardo might have said the same – and he actually did : 'It is a wretched pupil,' he wrote, 'who does not surpass his master.' Dürer and others expressed similar opinions. But if we take them literally, we again land in absurdity. What they evidently meant was that during the period of explosive development which started with Giotto around the year 1300, each successive generation of painters had discovered new tricks and techniques – foreshortening, perspective, the treatment of light, colour and texture, the capture of movement and facial expression – inventions which the pupil could take over from the master and use as his base-line for new departures.

But two qualifications come immediately to mind. The first is that this cumulative growth refers to the accretion of technical skills, and can only be called 'progress' if technical perfection is your criterion of judging a work of art. If your criteria are different, you may prefer archaic Greek figures to Golden Age statuary, or the Italian Primitives to the High Renaissance. The second objection to Leonardo's optimism is that it applies only to certain periods and not to others. In the whole history of Western art, there are two outstanding periods in which we find rapid, sustained, cumulative progress in representing nature, as tangible as the progress in engineering. The first stretches roughly from the middle of the 6th to the middle of the 4th century B.C., the second from the beginning of the fourteenth to the middle of the sixteenth century. Each lasted for about six to eight generations, in the course of which each giant did indeed stand on the shoulders of his predecessors, and could take in a wider view. It would of course be silly to say that these were the *only* periods of cumulative progress and to ignore, for instance, the visual discoveries of the Impressionists. But it is nevertheless true that in between these periods of rapid evolution there are much longer stretches of stagnation and decline. Besides, there are the *Einzelgänger*, the lone giants, who seem to appear from nowhere and cannot be fitted into any neat pyramid of acrobats balancing on each other's shoulders in the circus of history.

What are we to conclude? I think we ought to conclude that Nerzhin is certainly wrong – that there *is* progress in art in a limited sense, in limited directions during limited periods. But these short, luminous trails sooner or later peter out, and all around them there is twilight and confusion.

There is, however, comfort in the thought that the historical chart of the evolution of science does not offer a more coherent picture. When Nerzhin points to the contrast between the development of painting and that of technology since Rembrandt's day, he cheats, because the cumulative growth of science happens to start precisely in Rembrandt's century, which is also the century of Galileo, Kepler and Newton – but not before. It was only during these last 300 years or thereabouts that the progress of science has been continuous and cumulative; but those unfamiliar with the history of science – and they include the majority of scientists – tend to fall into the mistaken belief that the acquisition of knowledge has always been a neat and tidy ascent along a straight path towards the ultimate peak.

In fact, however, neither art nor science have evolved in a continuous way. Whitehead once remarked that Europe in

the year 1500 knew less than Archimedes who died in the
year 212 B.C. In retrospect there was only one step separating
Archimedes from Galileo, or Aristarchus of Samos from
Copernicus. But that step took nearly 2000 years to be made.
During that long period, science was hibernating. After the
three short glorious centuries of Greek science, roughly coin-
ciding with the cumulative period of Greek art, comes a
period of hibernation about six times as long; then a new
furious awakening, so far only about ten generations old.
And even during the luminous periods, when logical object-
ivity and detached reasoning were supposed to have prevailed, history echoes with the sound and fury of scientific
controveries even more venomous than the squabbles among
literati. It's a comfort.

Progress, then, in science as in art, is neither steady nor
absolute, but progress in a limited sense during limited
periods in limited directions; not along a steady curve, but in
a jagged, jerky, zigzag line. And yet I believe that it is possible
to detect a recurrent rhythm or pattern in the evolution of
both science and art. Think, for instance, of the succession
of major literary trends in Western Europe in the course of
the last two centuries: classicism; romanticism and *Sturm und
Drang*; the naturalistic novel; surrealism and Dada; the
socially conscious novel; the slice-of-life novel; existentialism;
the *nouveau roman*. It is of course impossible to isolate in the
strict sense any literary movement or school of thought;
there is always interaction and overlap; but nevertheless each
of these movements had an individual profile and life-cycle.

As a rule the life-cycle starts with a passionate rebellion
against, and rejection of, the previous dominant school, and a
breakthrough towards new frontiers. The second phase in the
cycle moves through a climate of optimism and euphoria in
the footsteps of the conquering giants. Their followers move
into the newly opened territories to explore and exploit its
rich potentials. This is the phase *par excellence* of the cumulative progress described earlier on; a time for consolidating
new insights, for elaborating and perfecting new styles and

techniques. The third phase brings saturation, followed by frustration and decline. The fourth and last phase is a time of desperate experimentation and anarchy, which prepares the next revolution, initiating a new departure in a new direction, and so the cycle starts again.

Let me, briefly, dwell on the first phase. The French Revolution demolished the Bastille and used its huge stones to pave the Place de la Concorde. In other words, revolutions are both destructive and constructive. Old restraints and conventions are discarded, aspects of human experience previously neglected or repressed are suddenly highlighted, there is a shift of emphasis, a reshuffling of data, a reordering of the hierarchy of values and of the criteria of relevance. This is what happened at each of the turning-points of narrative prose styles – classicism to romanticism, naturalism, and so on. This is what happened in the succession of dramatic changes in the artist's perception of the human body, from Egyptian painting to Picasso; or in the poet's view of the relation between the sexes; or the painter's attitude to nature. Throughout the Renaissance, for instance, and up to the late Venetians, landscapes were conceived merely as more or less stereotyped backdrops for the human figures on the stage. Art historians appear to agree that Giorgione's 'Tempest' is the first European painting in which nature claims to be seen in her own right – the violent thunderstorm in the background competes for our attention with the bucolic scene in the foreground.

Literature was even slower in coming to grips with nature in the raw. In his *History of Modern Aesthetics*, Listowel wrote:

Considering the bulk and value of Greek literature, and the artistic brilliance of Athens, the feeling for nature . . . was but poorly developed among a people whose achievement in the dramatic and sculptural arts has been unsurpassed; it is seriously lacking in Homer . . . and it can hardly be said to enter Greek drama . . . Indeed, the continent of nature had to wait for a thorough and minute exploration until the romantic movement of the nineteenth century: Byron, Shelley, Wordsworth, Goethe, first brought the ocean, the rivers and the mountain ranges into their own.[2]

Even Dr Johnson dismissed mountains as 'rather uncouth objects'.

This does not mean that artists who painted before Giorgione were blind to nature, or that poets before the romantic movement were lacking in emotive response. But their vision and response were different from ours, moulded by the *Zeitgeist*, just as successive schools of philosophers put different interpretations on the same data. To Homer a storm at sea signified the fury of Poseidon, and the dawn was painted by the rosy fingers of Aurora; to Virgil nature appeared tame and bucolic; it took quite a series of revolutionary shifts of emphasis and reshuffling of data until people learnt to see an apple through Cézanne's eye or a snow-covered plain through the eyes of Verlaine. And the adjective 'revolutionary' is no exaggeration, although in retrospect these revolutions seem quite tame. Verlaine, for instance, does not seem to have been unduly audacious when he compared the uncertain colour of the snow to luminous sand covering the 'interminable boredom of the plain', and the sky to dull copper in which the moon 'lived and died'. Today French school-children have to learn this poem by heart. But when it was published, a famous writer and critic attacked Verlaine in the shrill voice of the literary fishwife:

How can the moon live and die in a copper heaven? And how can snow shine like sand? How can the French attribute such importance to this versifier who is far from skilful in form and most contemptible and commonplace in subject-matter?

The fishwife was Count Leo Tolstoy; the source of the quotation is his once-celebrated essay, 'What is Art?'

If we try to define what these revolutions in different ages and in different art forms have in common, I would suggest that the one obvious feature they all share is a radical *shift in selective emphasis*. The artist, as the scientist, is engaged in projecting his vision of reality into a particular medium, whether the medium is paint, marble, words or mathematical equations. But the product of his efforts can never be an exact copy of reality, even if he naïvely hopes to achieve one.

In the first place, he is up against the peculiarities and limitations of his medium: the painter's canvas does not have the micro-structure of the human retina, stone lacks the plasticity of living tissue, words are symbols which do not smell, smile or bleed. In the second place, the artist's perception and outlook on the world also has its peculiarities and limitations imposed by the implicit conventions of his time. The two factors interact: there is continuous feedback from language to thought, from the clay under the sculptor's fingers to the image he is trying to materialize. The dynamic tension between the biased mind and the obstinate medium compels the artist to make decisions at every step he takes (though the decision-making need not be conscious): to select and emphasize those features of reality which he considers to be significant and to ignore those which he considers irrelevant. Some aspects of experience defy representation, some can only be rendered in a simplified or distorted way, some only at the price of sacrificing others.

The term 'selective emphasis' thus always involves three related factors: selection, exaggeration and simplification. They are at work in every province of art: in the narrative of events, historic or fictitious; in the visual representation of landscape or human figure, in portrait and caricature. But selective emphasis also operates in the scientist's laboratory. Every geographical map, every statistical diagram, every theoretical model of man or the universe is a deliberately schematized caricature of reality, based on the technique of selecting and highlighting the relevant features, simplifying or ignoring others according to the criteria of relevance of that particular discipline or school of thought. In psychology, for instance, one finds radically different criteria of relevance among nineteenth-century introspectionists, contemporary behaviourists, Freudians, Jungians and existential psychologists, with corresponding contrasts in selective emphasis, resulting in radically different portraits of man; and the same considerations apply to the history of medicine. In physics, the paradigm of exact science, there are radical shifts from Aristotelian anthropomorphism to Newtonian mechanism, from the deterministic to the probabilistic approach, from forces to fields. Even a cursory glance at the history of science makes one realize that its criteria of relevance are liable to changes as striking as the changes of style in art; and comparisons between the two domains make the history of art appear a little less confusing, by showing us at least a dim outline of a more comprehensible pattern.

Thus the recurrent revolutionary upheavals in the content and style of literary productions can be described as shifts in the criteria of relevance and in selective emphasis. The *second* phase in the historic cycle is the exploration of the new subject-matter, the elaboration of the new styles and techniques, which need not detain us here. For it is the *third* phase in the cycle which is of special interest to (and the main headache of) every practitioner of our profession: the phase of saturation and subsequent frustration of the writer and his audience. I quoted Tolstoy's indignant outcry against Verlaine's moon dying in a copper sky; today it is hard to understand what Tolstoy got so excited about. Yesterday's daring metaphors are today's clichés. Yesterday's obscenities are today's banalities, the bourgeois is no longer *épatable*; stark sex, like the moon deprived of its mystery, turns out to be all craters and pimples.

These are inevitable consequences of a fundamental property of the nervous system. Seasoned ambulance crews no longer turn a hair at the sight of mangled casualties, and even the inmates of Auschwitz developed a degree of emotional immunity. There exists a phenomenon which psychologists call habituation. You do not hear the ticking of the clock in your room, but you hear that it has suddenly stopped. You do not feel the pressure of the chair against your back; but you do feel it when you shift your position. Nerve cells in the retina do not signal sameness, they only signal contrast. And habituation is not confined to man. Dr Horn at Cambridge has recently found single nerve cells in the mid-brain of a rabbit which respond promptly to a tone sounded at a frequency of 1000 cycles per second, but cease to respond after several repetitions of the stimulus. Habituation to the 1000-cycle tone does not, however, prevent a strong response of the same cell when an only slightly different, 900-cycle tone is sounded. Dr Horn presented examples of similar phenomena in animals as different as locusts, squids and cats.[3]

If even a squid can be that blasé, how can the writer hope to fight the law of diminishing returns? The recurrent cycles of stagnation, crisis, revolution and new departure seem to be mainly caused by the progressive habituation of both artist and audience to any well-established technique, style or subject-matter, and its resulting loss of emotional appeal, of evocative power. This loss, unfortunately, is unavoidable, because once the new style has become stabilized and familiar, the reader no longer needs to exert his imagination to assimilate the message; he is deprived of the effort or re-creation and degraded to a mere consumer. There can be little doubt that the bulk of all literature, probably from Greece onwards, but certainly since the invention of the printing press, consisted of inferior consumer goods, written in the long periods of stagnation within the recurrent cycle. But this huge mass of pulp has decayed and vanished from sight; only samples of exceptional quality have survived and provide the material of the history of literature.

Any new art form, however revolutionary it seemed at first, grows after a while tired and stale; it loses its power over the audience. The staleness lies of course not in the form itself, which may be enduring, but in the consumer's jaded palate. In 1933, at the peak of the great Soviet famine, the co-operative store for foreign specialists in Kharkhov had practically nothing for sale except caviar. For several months I lived on a pound of caviar a day; you can imagine the result. The history of art could be written in terms of the artist's struggle against the deadening effects of saturation. It is not his fault if he is fighting a losing battle. He may produce cheese-cake or he may produce caviar, he is nevertheless helpless against the fundamental process of habituation which operates in the rabbit's brain as in the reader's nervous system. Its effect on the artist is a growing sense of frustration, and the growing realization – which may be conscious or not – that the conventional techniques of his time have become inadequate as a medium of communication and self-expression.

Two opposite methods seem to have been tried over and again to improve communication with the audience: screaming and whispering. The first tries to impress the message on the audience by an overly direct appeal to the emotions, through tear-jerkers, melodramatics or more refined derivations of it; it tries to provide spicier fare for jaded appetites and to cover impotence by flamboyant gestures and mannerisms. In the visual arts one finds some or all of these symptoms cropping up in the successive periods of decline of Egyptian, Greek and Roman sculpture, in the manneristic styles of the late Baroque, in the choicer horrors of the Victorian age, and so on. The general trend in periods of decadence is towards the over-emphatic and the over-explicit, and need not concern us further.

The opposite method to counteract diminishing returns in the evolution of art is of much greater interest. Instead of relying on the emphatic and the explicit, it tends towards economy and implicitness. It is usual to credit the French Symbolist movement – Mallarmé, Verlaine, Rimbaud – with having initiated the shift from explicit statement to implicit suggestion, and the French Impressionist school with a parallel achievement in painting. However, this movement from the obvious to the oblique can be observed in the most varied periods and art forms as an effective antidote to satiety and decadence. Nevertheless it is worth quoting a passage in which Mallarmé outlines the programme of the Symbolist movement:

It seems to me that there should be only allusions. The volatile image of the dreams they evoke, these make the song: the Parnassians [the classicist movement of Leconte de Lisle, Heredia, *et al.*] who make a complete demonstration of the object thereby lack mystery; *they deprive the [reader's] mind of that delicious joy of imagining that it creates.* To *name* the thing means foresaking three-quarters of a poem's enjoyment – which is derived from unravelling it gradually, by happy guesswork: to *suggest* the thing creates the dream.[4]

Yet this technique was not invented by the symbolists; it is as old as art itself. It starts with mythology. The *Baghavad Gita* is an allegory which every Hindu scholar and mystic interprets after his own fashion; Genesis is studded with archetypal symbols; Christ speaks in parables, the Oracle in riddles, Orpheus on fiddles. The purpose is not to obscure the message; on the contrary, it is to make it more luminous by compelling the recipient to act as a flourescent screen, to work out the implications by his own effort, to re-create it. 'Implicit' is derived from the Latin *plicare*, and means 'folded in,' like a roll of parchment. The implicit message has to be unfolded by the reader; he must unravel it, fill the gaps, solve riddles. But as time goes by, the reader learns to see through the tricks, the disguises became transparent, he is deprived, as Mallarmé has it, 'of that delicious joy of imagining that he creates'. So the writer or poet will strive towards even more disciplined economy and more subtle implications; the parchment will be rolled in even tighter.

I once called this 'the law of infolding'[5]; it seems to be the most effective reply to the law of diminishing returns. It runs like a kind of leitmotiv through the history of literature.

The Homeric epics were originally broadcast by travelling bards who impersonated their heroes by voice and acting, which is the most direct and emphatic method of narration. Later on, around the seventh century B.C., the epics were consolidated in their present form, to be recited on festive occasions; by now, however, they were folded into rolls of parchment. The bard impersonated; the reciter imitated; the written word has to be deciphered. A pair of quotation marks are sufficient to symbolize the human voice, and printer's ink is generally more effective in arousing emotion than a histrionic recital. Histrionics are left to the stage and screen, but they are also subject to the law of infolding. Victorian melodrama has become a parody of its own genre, and films not more than twenty years old which moved us at the time appear now – exceptions always granted – surprisingly dated, too obvious, overacted, over-explicit. And the background music is simply incredible.

The writer's best friend is his pair of scissors. In his advice to a young writer Hemingway wrote: 'The more bloody good stuff you cut out, the more bloody good your novel will be . . .' The law of infolding demands that the reader should never be given something for nothing; he must be made to pay in emotional currency by exerting his imagination. Otherwise one gets the dreaded 'so what?' reaction. 'Caroline felt her heart go out to Peter.' So what? Let it go out. The German word for composing poetry is *dichten* – to compress. But compression can also operate in semantic space, by squeezing several meanings, or levels of meaning, into a single statement. Freud thought that this was the essence of poetry; Empson's 'seven types of ambiguity' are variations on the same theme. Needless to say, the techniques of infolding can be used in a fraudulent manner to create deliberate obscurity. Though it has been said that the Venus of Milo would lose much of her attraction if her arms were restored, it is unlikely that her creator broke them off in cold blood. But who can draw the line between deliberate cheating and the tricks of the unconscious? Much of the *nouveau roman* and of *Last*

Year in Marienbad reminds one of a way of playing poker where you hide your cards not only from your opponent but from yourself. This can sometimes be a winning strategy – but what does 'winning' mean in this context?

There are many other fields where one can watch the law of infolding at work. Humour for instance has travelled a long way from the *Punch* cartoon to the *New Yorker's* sophisticated riddles. Metaphors have a way of shrivelling into dehydrated clichés; they are replaced by fresh supplies of a less obvious and explicit kind. Rhythm and metre have evolved from simple, repetitive pulses into intricate patterns, in which the erstwhile beat of the tom-tom is implied, but no longer pounded out. Rhyme, as the most explicit form of euphony, is folding in – or up.

In the contemporary visual arts the process is too obvious to need stressing. Only a forger could, in our day, paint in the style of Vermeer (however perfect his technique) because to paint like Vermeer, the artist would have to forget that he has ever seen a Manet or Cézanne. So he has to be either a forger or a Rip Van Winkle who has slept since the seventeenth century. But it would be a mistake to believe that the trend towards the implicit is found only in modern painting. Leonardo invented the technique of the *sfumato* or veiled form, such as the blurred contours at the corners of the Mona Lisa's eyes, which have never lost their fascination; and Titian in his old age invented the technique of what Vasari called 'the crudely daubed strokes and blobs' which, looked at from close quarters, cannot be deciphered and which let the picture unfold only when you step back; Rembrandt went through a similar progression, from the neat and meticulous to the loose and suggestive brushstroke in his rendering of embroideries. The examples could be multiplied. It could be said, for instance, that in the peak periods of Chinese painting the picture consisted of what was left out. I cannot resist quoting just one phrase from a seventeenth-century Chinese manual (which I owe to Gombrich): 'Figures even though painted without eyes, must seem to look; without ears, must seem to listen . . . That is truly giving expression to the invisible . . .'

To make a last cross-reference to science, even there the law of infolding operates. Aristotle firmly believed that all possible discoveries and inventions had already been made in his time; Bacon and Descartes thought that it would take just one more generation to solve all the mysteries of the universe; even nineteenth-century scientists held such optimistic beliefs. Only recently did we begin to realize that the unfolding of the secrets of nature was accompanied by a parallel process of infolding, because the more precise knowledge the physicist acquired, the more ambiguous and elusive the mathematical symbols he had to use; he could no longer make an intelligible model of reality, he could only allude to it by abstract equations.

To sum up – I have tried to point to a recurrent pattern in the history of science and art which, broadly speaking, both seem to move through cycles of Revolution – Consolidation – Saturation – Crisis and New Departure. Revolutions are characterized by shifts in selective emphasis; the period of consolidation is one of cumulative progress; the third period is a constant struggle against the law of diminishing returns, and one of the effective antidotes is indicated by the law of infolding. I must ask your indulgence for so much law-making and speculation; but if the Creator had a purpose in equipping us with a neck, he surely meant us to stick it out.

REFERENCES

1. E. H. Gombrich, *Art and Illusion* (London, 1962), pp. 9, 120.
2. W. F. H. Listowel, *A Critical History of Modern Aesthetics* (1933), p. 217.
3. *New Scientist*, 7 August 1969.
4. S. Mallarmé, *Enquête sur l'Évolution Littéraire* (1888).
5. *The Act of Creation* (London, 1964).

Science and Para-Science*

In the 1950s a remarkable periodical was published in England by the physicist Dr Irving John Good, called the *Journal of Half-Baked Ideas*. A selection of articles from it was later published as a book with the title: *The Scientist Speculates: An Anthology of Partly Baked Ideas.*[1] The paper I am about to deliver is a sort of club sandwich of partly baked ideas, which has several layers. The top layer, on which I shall start, is a fully baked crust which through long exposure has almost hardened into clichés. The subsequent layers will be half-baked, quarter-baked, and so on, until we reach the bottom layer of shamelessly raw speculation.

In a recently published book[2] I tried to make the point that the unthinkable phenomena of parapsychology appear somewhat less preposterous in the light of the unthinkable propositions of modern quantum physics. This argument is by no means new; it has been so often and so brilliantly demonstrated that it has almost become a commonplace. But it can also be applied, less fashionably, to classical pre-Heisenberg physics. To mention a single example: from the point of view of naïve common sense, the type of action-at-a-distance called telepathy is no more mysterious than that

---

* Banquet Address to the Annual Convention of the Parapsychological Association, Edinburgh, September 1972. Parts of this paper I have incorporated in *The Challenge of Chance: Experiments and Speculations* by Sir Alister Hardy, Robert Harvie and myself (London and New York, 1973).

other action-at-a-distance called universal gravity. When Kepler, eighty years before Newton, came out with the wild suggestion that the tides were caused by the attraction of the moon, even Galileo dismissed the idea as an occult fancy, which contradicted the laws of nature. And Newton himself vehemently rejected the concept of universal gravity *unless* there existed some interstellar medium which transmitted it. In his third letter to Bentley he wrote: 'That one body may act upon another, at a distance, through a vacuum, without the mediation of anything else . . . is to me so great an absurdity that no man who has . . . a competent faculty of thinking can ever fall into it.'

Yet fall we all did, as schoolboys in the classroom, without becoming aware of our fallen state. Such is the power of mental habituation. To live with a paradox is like being married to a nagging bitch; after a while you become deaf to her nagging and settle down in comfortable resignation.

Thus even classical physics could only make progress at the price of insulting common sense and by breaking and re-making the previously sacrosanct laws of nature. Modern physics had to repeat both offences in even more brutal ways. And parapsychology has to carry a similar burden of guilt. Einstein, de Broglie and Schrödinger between them have de-materialized matter like the conjuror who makes the lady vanish from the box on the stage. Heisenberg replaced determinism by uncertainty and causality by statistics; Dirac postulated holes in space stuffed with electrons of negative mass; Thomson made a single particle go through two holes in a screen at the same time – which, Cyril Burt commented, is more than a ghost can do. Photons of zero rest-mass have been observed in the process of giving virgin birth to twins endowed with solid rest-mass; Feynman made time flow backwards on his diagrams; and these are but a few glimpses from the surrealistic panorama which quantum physics has opened up for us. To paraphrase an old saying: inside the atom is where things happen that don't.

The astronomers are having an equally gay time. The Big

Bang versus Continual Creation controversy would have delighted mediaeval theologians. Radio astronomers claim that they can hear background noises which must have originated with the pristine bang of creation. More recently the universe became pockmarked with black holes into which the mass of collapsing stars is sucked at the speed of light, to be annihilated and vanish from our universe into the blue yonder. The universe is turning out to be a very odd place indeed, and we no longer need ghosts to make our hair stand on end.

My purpose in reminding you of these well-known developments was to underline once more the fact that the mechanistic and deterministic world-view, which is still dominant in sociology, the behavioural sciences and in the public at large, no longer has a leg left to stand on; it has become a Victorian anachronism. The nineteenth-century clockwork model of the universe is in shambles, and since matter itself has been de-materialized, materialism can no longer claim to be a scientific philosophy.

As a side-effect of this philosophical crisis, we may observe a curiously reciprocal development in the exact sciences on the one hand, and parapsychology on the other. For the last fifty years, our leading physicists have been playing around with more and more obscure mental constructs, whose quasi-mystical implications are camouflaged by technical jargon and mathematical formalism. If Galileo were alive, he would certainly have accused them of dabbling in occult fancies. At the same time he might have looked with a benevolent eye at the parapsychologist's increasing reliance on hard statistics, rigorous controls, mechanical gadgets and electronic computers. Thus the intellectual climate in the two camps seems to have been changing in opposite directions: Rhine's successors, because of their statistical orientation, have sometimes been accused of scientific pedantry, while Einstein's successors were accused of flirting with ghosts in the guise of particles which possess no mass, nor weight, nor any precise location in space.

I believe that this apparent convergence is more than a surface phenomenon. But one must be careful in drawing conclusions from it. The time for physics and parapsychology to fall happily into each other's arms is not yet. What both have increasingly in common are the two negative attributes that I mentioned a minute ago: both defy common sense, and both defy the previously accepted laws of nature. They are both provocative and iconoclastic. And, to say it once more, the baffling paradoxes produced by one make the baffling paradoxes of the other appear a little less preposterous. If whole stars can vanish into black holes there may also be singularities in the continuum which produce poltergeists.

One might call this a kind of negative affinity. In concrete terms it does not amount to much. But philosophically and emotionally it seems to me significant. It helps to put one's nagging doubts at rest. It is encouraging to know that if the parapsychologist is out on a limb, the physicist is out on a tightrope.

But unavoidably the question arises whether there are any signs on the horizon of a *positive* affinity or convergence between post-materialistic physics and post-spiritualistic parapsychology? I think one can distinguish two such signposts, the first of a subjective, the second of an objective, nature.

An impressive number of eminent physicists, including several Nobel laureates, have shown an inclination to flirt with parapsychology – witnessed by the list of past presidents of the Society for Psychic Research; and, as in other subversive movements, the number of fellow travellers far exceeds that of the card-carrying members. Thus the discoverer of the electron, Sir Joseph J. Thomson, was one of the earliest members of the Society. Now why should physicists in particular show this proneness to infection by the E.S.P. bug? The answer can be found in the autobiographical writings and metaphysical speculations of the greatest among them. The dominant chord which you can detect in nearly all of them is a pervasive feeling of frustration, based on the realization that science can only elucidate certain aspects or levels of reality, while the ultimate questions will always elude its grasp, vanishing into infinite regress like images reflected in a hall of mirrors. 'Physics is mathematical,' wrote Bertrand Russell, 'not because we know so much about the physical world, but because we know so little; it is only its mathematical properties that we can discover.'[3] This resigned agnosticism leads either into a spiritual desert – Schrödinger in his middle age gave up physics in disgust – or, more often, it leads to a new open-mindedness, a sophisticated kind of innocence on a higher turn of the spiral.

So much about what I have called the subjective aspect of convergence. The next step is to look for *objective* convergences, i.e., areas where the domains of physics and parapsychology might enter into direct contact. But this step means digging into a deeper layer of the club sandwich, which is no longer fully baked. There is no need to dwell here on earlier abortive efforts to provide a physical explanation of E.S.P. by radio-waves and the like. They were honourable attempts at dressing the wolf in sheep's clothing, and inevitably failed. With the advent of quantum theory, however, these attempts became considerably more sophisticated – we might say that they progressed from the quarter-baked to the half-baked stage. Examples are Axel Firsoff's hypothesis of extrasensory communication by means of *mindons* – the hypothetical particles of an all-pervasive mind-stuff, with properties somewhat similar to the neutrino's; Martin Ruderfer's complex theory of a neutrino sea interacting with matter; and the late Adrian Dobbs's *psitrons*, swarms of particles of imaginary mass, travelling along a second, imaginary time dimension, and capable of impinging directly on neurons in the percipients' brains.

These theories are of considerable ingenuity, and I do not think that physicists could find any obvious fault with them. Yet, like other similar efforts, they fail to satisfy because they give the impression of improvised bridges across the nasty abyss, supported by *ad hoc* hypotheses. One cannot help feeling that these imaginative efforts are stimulating but premature, and that they suffer from what Whitehead called 'misplaced concreteness'. To put it differently, their authors seem to remain under the spell of the physicist's concepts and categories, instead of creating their own, autonomous conceptual systems, a universe of discourse commensurate with the phenomena in their own field – as biology has done to some extent. I would like to quote here another after-dinner speaker at one of your earlier conventions, the Professor of Physics at Yale:

I have probed physics for suggestions it can offer towards a solution of the sort of problem you seem to encounter. The positive results, I fear, are meagre and disappointing ... But why, I should like to ask, is it necessary to import into any new discipline all the approved concepts of an older science in its contemporary stage of development? Physics did not adhere slavishly to the Greek rationalistic formulations that preceded it; it was forced to create its own specific constructs ...

The parapsychologist, I think ... must strike out on his own and probably reason in bolder terms than present-day physics suggest.[4]

This does not mean of course that parapsychology should cut itself off from the mainstream of scientific research, and retire into an ivory tower. But that mainstream itself is now flowing into bold new directions which seem to point to an indirect sort of convergence in the future – not by premature short cuts, but by a sort of isomorphism or Gestalt affinity. I am referring here to what one might call the *mentalistic trend* in biology and physics with its explicit or implied admission of the power of mind over matter. This trend seems to be an indirect consequence of those paradoxical developments in physics which I have mentioned before. In its still early days, Sir James Jeans made his celebrated *pronunciamento*: 'Today there is a wide measure of agreement, which on the physical side of science approaches almost to unanimity, that the stream of knowledge is heading towards a non-mechanical reality; the universe begins to look more like a great thought than a great machine.'[5]

This statement was not meant as a poetic metaphor; it was the embarrassing but inescapable conclusion emerging from the physical laboratories. There were several aspects to it. One of the most fundamental was the principle of complementarity. It stated that the smallest constituents of the universe are ambiguous, Janus-faced entities which under certain conditions behave like hard little pellets, under other conditions like waves in a non-material medium. These two types of behaviour mutually exclude each other, but also mutually complement each other. Heisenberg was apparently the first to recognize that this complementarity may be regarded as a paradigm of the dualism of matter and mind. In his autobiography he was even more explicit. 'Atoms are not *things*,' he wrote. 'When we get down to the atomic level, the objective world in space and time no longer exists.'[6] From here there is only one step to the realization that the contents of mental experience also defy definition in terms of space, time and substance, yet are somehow linked with the material brain – as the wave-function of the electron is somehow linked with its material aspect. One might conclude, with Dr Good (in *The Scientist Speculates*) that 'the physicist's basic wave equation – Schrödinger's psi function – is mysterious enough to provoke the conjecture that it may in some sense explain features of the mind. Perhaps the psi of quantum physics depends on the psi of the parapsychologists.' Other scientists have pointed half jokingly, half seriously, at the hidden sympathies between the two psis.

Thus there is not only a *negative* convergence between the two domains in the sense of a shared contempt for common sense and for mental smugness; there are also portents of a tentative *positive* convergence – which, however, is more implicit than explicit, potential rather than actual, intuitive rather than logical – a sort of Gestalt affinity as I called it before. It should not be hurried or forced; I am old-fashioned enough to believe that courtship should precede copulation.

The great syntheses in the history of thought emerge when the time is ripe for them – when all the components which are to go into the new synthesis are already present. Neither science nor parascience appears to have reached that stage.

One might add here, as a footnote, that in biology too there is a growing tendency to recognize the power of mind over matter. Some twenty years ago Sir John Eccles created quite a stir when he proposed that the exercise of conscious volition – a dirty word in behaviouristic psychology – could, by affecting a single neuron, trigger off changes of activity in large areas of the cortical network. Since then, other researchers have shown that mental volition, assisted by various types of biofeedback apparatus, can influence the activities of the autonomous nervous system and bring on the alpha-wave rhythm of the brain.

We have now arrived at the last layer of the club sandwich which is almost completely unbaked. I am approaching it with a certain amount of trepidation. The more so as I must now revert to some anecdotal material – which, however, may come as a relief after so much quantum jabberwocky.

When my recent book, *The Roots of Coincidence*, was published, I received a good many letters from people anxious to relate their experiences. I shall quote from two of these, which seem to me remarkable in their different ways.

The contents of the first I must relate in a slightly camouflaged version to spare the feelings of those involved. It concerns a young architect who had suffered a nervous breakdown and thrown himself in front of an incoming train in a London tube station. He suffered a fractured pelvis, punctured abdomen with extrusion of intestine, lacerated back and severe bruising, but survived. They had to jack up the train to get him out; he had been under it, but the wheels had stopped just short of his body. However, according to the hospital doctor's account to the victim's relatives, which was later confirmed by an official of London Transport, the train was not stopped by the driver applying the brakes (the time-lag was apparently too short for that) but because a passenger in the train, quite unaware of what was happening, had pulled the emergency handle.

I passed the case on to a friend who was willing to investigate it – Mr Tom Tickell, who works on the editorial staff of the *Guardian*. Mr Tickell contacted London Transport, but ran into the traditional barrier of red tape. The identity of the passenger who had pulled the emergency handle was allegedly unknown. The name of the driver of the train was eventually disclosed, but not his address. A letter to the driver, addressed c/o London Transport, remained unanswered. Thus, as so often happens, the case petered out.*

The next case is in a different vein. What follows is an extract from a letter from J. B. Priestley, after he had read my book. No doubt you know that Priestley is married to Jacquetta Hawkes, the archaeologist.

My wife bought three large coloured lithographs by Graham Sutherland. When they arrived here from London she took them up to her bedroom, to hang them up in the morning. They were leaning against a chair and the one on the outside, facing the room, was a lithograph of a grasshopper. When Jacquetta got into bed that night, she felt some sort of twittering movement going on, so she got out and pulled back the clothes. There was a grasshopper in the bed. No grasshopper had been seen in that room before, nor has been seen since. No grasshopper has ever been seen at any other time in this house.[8]

The first of these stories might possibly be explained by E.S.P. which prompted the unknown passenger to pull the emergency handle; the second, in common with many coincidental happenings, defies explanation in both conventional and parapsychological terms. They are equally baffling to the theologian, for if the passenger's action is to be credited to Providence, what prompted Providence to put a

---

* For a more detailed description of it, see *The Challenge of Chance*.[7]

grasshopper in Mrs Priestley's bed? I have never heard it suggested that Providence has a sense of humour.

Whether one believes that such highly improbable meaningful coincidences are manifestations of some unknown principle operating beyond physical causality, or are produced by the proverbial monkey at the typewriter, is a matter of inclination and temperament. I have found to my surprise that the majority of my acquaintances – among whom scientists predominate – belong to the former category, although some are reluctant to confess it, for fear of ridicule, even to themselves. Carl Jung had the same experience among his patients, which was perhaps not surprising; more surprising is that Nobel laureate Wolfgang Pauli (one of the chief architects of quantum theory, who predicted the existence of the neutrino) co-operated with Jung on the latter's famous treatise: 'Synchronicity: An Acausal Connecting Principle'.[9] Jung defines synchronicity as 'the simultaneous occurrence of two or more meaningfully but not causally connected events'; and the a-causal factor behind such events is said to be *'equal in rank to causality as a principle of explanation'*.

The origins of Jung–Pauli's synchronicity concept can be traced back partly to Schopenhauer, partly to the Austrian biologist Paul Kammerer who, in 1919, published a book (which put an end to his academic career) called *Das Gesetz der Serie*[10] (not translated). Kammerer's concept of Seriality referred to the recurrence or clustering of meaningfully but not causally connected events – familiar to all gamblers and insurance companies. He postulated that coexistent with causality there is an a-causal principle active in the universe which tends towards unity. It is in some respects comparable to universal gravity, but whereas gravity acts indiscriminately on inert mass, this force correlates by affinity, or a kind of selective resonance. 'We thus arrive,' he writes, 'at the image of a world-mosiac or cosmic kaleidoscope, which, in spite of constant shufflings and rearrangements, also takes care of bringing like and like together.'

Now this sounds pretty wild talk in the twentieth century, but in fact the concept goes back all the way to the Hippo-cratic 'sympathy of all things': 'there is one common flow, one common breathing, all things are in sympathy'. This doctrine that everything in the universe is hanging together, not by mechanical causes but by hidden affinities which account for apparent coincidences, was not only the founda-tion of primitive magic, of astrology and alchemy; it also runs as a leitmotiv through the teachings of the Pythagoreans, Neoplatonists and the philosophers of the early Renaissance. Jung's dualism of causality and a-causal synchronicity was neatly formulated by Pico della Mirandola, *anno domini* 1550:

Firstly there is the unity in things whereby each thing is at one with itself, consists of itself, and coheres with itself. Secondly, there is the unity whereby one creature is united with the others and all parts of the world constitute one world.[11]

The scientific revolution put an end to this type of thinking and proclaimed mechanical causality as the absolute ruler of matter and mind. Yet three centuries later we are witnessing a swing of the pendulum in the opposite direction. On the quantum level the absolute rule of causality has come to an end; and Schrödinger's psi function, which defines a single electron, is spread out, Mirandola-wise, over the whole universe. On the cosmic scale Mach's principle, endorsed by Einstein, stipulates that the inertial forces on earth are governed by the total mass of the universe around us. Whitehead commented:

It is difficult to take seriously the suggestion that these domestic phenomena on the earth are due to the influence of the fixed stars. I cannot persuade myself to believe that a little star in its twinkling turned round Foucault's pendulum in the Paris Exhibition of 1851.[12]

But there it is. Mach's principle has become an integral part of modern physics, even though it smacks of the Hippo-cratic 'sympathy of all things'. For it implies not only that the universe at large influences local events, but also that local events have an influence, however small, on the universe at large. Everything hangs together; microcosm reflects macrocosm and is reflected by it.

In biology, too, there is a search for new principles – or, perhaps, a revival of earlier insights – which would offer a more satisfying approach to the creative aspects of evolution than Neo-Darwinism, for all its historic merits, has been able to provide. Jacques Monod's *Chance and Necessity* (1971) may turn out to be the swan-song of a rash generation of scientists who claimed that chance mutations plus natural selection provide the *complete* explanation of the emergence of higher levels of organization, of more complex structures and forms of behaviour. Today more and more biologists are coming to realize that random mutations may provide part of the explanation, but not the whole explanation, and perhaps not even an important part of it.

At the same time, the tyranny of the Second Law of Thermodynamics with its implied tendency towards transforming cosmos into chaos seems to be approaching its end, with the realization that the law applies only to so-called closed systems, whereas in open systems such as a living organism, an opposite tendency seems to be at work – creating order out of disorder, cosmos out of chaos, designing patterns where none existed before. This ubiquitous constructive principle has been proposed by various authors under various names; it carries echoes of Galen's and Kepler's *facultas formatrix*, Goethe's *Gestaltung* and Bergson's *élan vital*; in more recent times the German biologist Woltereck proposed the term 'anamorphosis', which von Bertalanffy adopted, while L. L. Whyte called it the 'morphic principle'. It is related to Schrödinger's concept of organisms feeding on negative entropy, which again is related to what I called elsewhere the Integrative Tendency.[2]

What all these tentative formulations have in common is that they regard the morphic, or formative, or Integrative Tendency, the striving towards higher forms of unity-in-diversity, as an essential factor in biological and mental evolution, and as an irreducible principle, which is as fundamental to the sciences of life as its antagonist, the Second Law of Thermodynamics, is to inanimate matter. Whether you call such a principle causal or a-causal is a matter of semantics.

I would like to end this talk by mentioning briefly two somewhat bizarre, way-out experiments. A young graduate student named Stuart Kaufman at California Medical School created quite a stir some four or five years ago by setting up a system of several hundred simple binary on-off switches; each switch had the inputs coming into it from two other switches chosen at random; and each input channel had one of the functions of Boolean logic – yes, no, and, or – assigned to it, again at random. Then he fed an electric impulse into that chaotic system and watched what was going to happen. What happened was that the system soon settled down into a cyclic routine, the impulses going round in a complex stable pattern, or one of several alternative patterns – order had been generated from disorder. What's more, when the system's routine was disturbed, the pattern soon righted itself – the originally random system manifested a kind of homeostasis.[13]

The second experiment is something of a skeleton in the cupboard of the British S.P.R. I am referring to the famous Spencer Brown controversy of twenty years ago. Brown claimed that by matching pairs of digits at random, the first digit symbolizing an E.S.P. guess, the second the target card, he obtained a significantly higher number of 'hits' than chance expectation. Mr Arthur T. Oram, an expert statistician, aided by several volunteer workers, then undertook the task of verifying Brown's results. His team matched no less than 500,000 digits taken from random tables. The result was strictly according to chance expectation, so Spencer Brown was refuted and all seemed well. But then Spencer Brown made a thorough analysis of Oram's tables – and discovered the classic decline effect of hits with odds against chance of the order of 7,000 to one.[14] It should be pointed out that

Brown did not question the validity of the results obtained by E.S.P. experiments – which he accepted at face value; but he thought that they pointed to some anomaly or hidden factor in the very nature or randomness. He did not elaborate on the nature of this suspected anomaly, but the idea bears a close resemblance to Kammerer's Seriality and Jung–Pauli's synchronicity – the morphic or patterning or Integrative Tendency invading even the sober realm of random tables – as it invaded Kaufmann's anarchic random circuits. It seems that nature is fond of blowing smoke-rings.

Sir Alister Hardy, in his Gifford Lectures, seems inclined to believe that Spencer Brown was on the right track. This, he pointed out, would by no means invalidate the evidence for 'true' E.S.P. in spontaneous cases and also in *some* laboratory experiments. But he surmised that the results of a certain number of card-guessing and other statistical experiments

may be due to something quite different from telepathy . . . something no less fundamental and interesting . . . something implicit in the very nature and meaning of randomness itself . . . Let me say that if some of this apparent card-guessing and dice-influencing work should in fact turn out to be something very different, it will not, I believe, have been a wasted effort; it will have provided a wonderful mine of material for the study of a very remarkable new principle.[15]

I may add that Hardy himself has in the meantime produced a substantial body of evidence, to be published shortly,[7] for that hypothetical new principle – which dates back, as I said, to Hippocrates. It seems to be guided by E. M. Forster's motto: connect, always connect. How it works we do not know. We only know that it cannot work within the framework of classical causality any more than the quantum phenomena can be fitted into it. Perhaps it is somehow related to the physicist's 'god of the gaps.' Perhaps the roots of coincidence sprout from those gaps. To try to explain by it how the grasshopper got into Mrs Priestley's bed would be a grotesque exercise in misplaced concreteness. But the little mystic who is hidden inside each great scientist, longing to be let out, may perceive a connection which earlier cultures have always taken for granted. If I were asked to sum up in a single sentence these half-baked ideas at the end of my talk, I would propose this paraphrase of Spinoza: 'Nature abhors randomness.'

REFERENCES

1. I. J. Good, ed., *The Scientist Speculates* (London, 1962).
2. A. Koestler, *The Roots of Coincidence* (London and New York, 1972).
3. Bertrand Russell, *An Outline of Philosophy* (London, 1927).
4. H. Margenau, in *Science and E.S.P.*, ed. J. R. Smythies (London, 1967).
5. Sir James Jeans, *The Mysterious Universe* (Cambridge, 1937).
6. W. Heisenberg, *Der Teil und das Ganze* (Munich, 1969).
7. Sir A. Hardy, R. Harvie and A. Koestler, *The Challenge of Chance* (London and New York, 1973).
8. J. B. Priestley, in a letter to A.K. dated 7 February 1972.
9. C. G. Jung, 'Synchronizität als ein Prinzip akausaler Zusammenhänge' in Jung–Pauli, *Naturerklärung und Psyche. Studien aus dem C. G. Jung-Institut, Zürich, IV*, 1952.
10. Paul Kammerer, *Das Gesetz der Serie* (Stuttgart and Berlin, 1919).
11. Pico della Mirandola, *Opera Omnia* (Basle, 1557).
12. Quoted by D. W. Sciama, *The Unity of the Universe* (London, 1959).
13. Stuart Kaufman, in *Journal of Theoretical Biology*, 1969.
14. G. Spencer Brown, *Probability and Scientific Inference* (London, 1957).
15. Sir Alister Hardy, *The Living Stream* (London, 1965).

Science and Reality*

Some of my friends and well-wishers professed to be shocked because my last book, *The Roots of Coincidence*, is concerned with parapsychology – i.e., telepathy and the even more puzzling phenomena of psychokinesis, short-term precognition and apparently meaningful coincidences. I would like to take this opportunity to mention briefly some of the reasons which may prompt a rational person – which I believe myself to be – with a strong scientific bent, to get involved in these unorthodox branches of research.

The evidence for E.S.P. can be divided into two broad categories – on the one hand experiments in the laboratory and on the other hand what one might call out-of-the-blue phenomena which occur spontaneously, such as veridical dreams, clocks which stop at the moment of a person's death, and other meaningful coincidences. Such events do not constitute scientific evidence, although a great many people have experienced them; however strong their emotional impact, rationality prompts us to attribute them to chance.

But the evidence produced in the laboratories cannot be thus dismissed. Any single event – like the stopping of that clock – however improbable, can be ascribed to chance because the laws of probability do not apply to single events,

* Broadcast Interview, National Broadcasting Company, New York, September 1972.

only to large numbers of events on a statistical scale. But probability statistics is precisely the method in modern E.S.P. laboratory research, based on the same type of calculation as that employed by physicists, geneticists, market-researchers and insurance companies. And the *same* logic which compels us to dismiss the stopping of the clock as a chance event also compels us to *exclude* the possibility of chance if a telepathic subject persistently, in thousands of consecutive card-guessing or dice-throwing experiments, scores a persistently higher number of hits than the probability calculus permits – because here the odds against chance are on an astronomical scale.

It was this strictly orthodox, statistical approach, applied to an unorthodox subject, which gradually wore down academic resistance – and incredulity – in the course of the forty years since Professor Rhine established the first Laboratory for Parapsychology at Duke University, North Carolina. Since then, a great number of similar laboratories have been established all over the world – including Soviet Russia and other Communist countries – in which scientists work under the same rigorously controlled test-conditions as researchers in other fields, using sophisticated computers and electronic apparatus to eliminate as far as possible human error in evaluating the results. And the results show that E.S.P. – extrasensory perception – is a fact, whether we like it or not. In 1969 the American Association for the Advancement of Science approved the application of the Parapsychological Association to become an associate of that august body. That decision conferred on parapsychology the ultimate seal of respectability.

Nevertheless, even open-minded people feel a strong intellectual discomfort, or even revulsion when confronted with phenomena which seem to contradict what they believe to be the immutable laws of physics. The answer is that the laws of physics are by no means immutable, but in constant flux; and that since the advent of Planck, Einstein and Heisenberg, modern quantum physics has discarded all our classical, commonsense notions of time, space, matter and causality. Thus both physics and parapsychology point to aspects or levels of reality beyond the reach of contemporary science – a coded message written in invisible ink between the lines of a banal letter. Though we can only decipher tantalizingly small fragments of the message, the knowledge that it is there is exciting and comforting at the same time.

Solitary Confinement*

ANTHONY GREY: I've been reading *Dialogue with Death* and some of your autobiography, *The Invisible Writing*, and I've been increasingly struck by the similarities between our experiences. You were arrested in 1937, and held in solitary confinement in Spain. Thirty years later in 1967 I was arrested and held in solitary confinement in China. We were both journalists. And campaigns were in both cases mounted at home for our release; and when we came home, we both wrote books. You wrote *Dialogue with Death* in two months, and I wrote *Hostage in Peking* in six weeks. We were both thirty-two. I'm thirty-two now, you were thirty-two then. And these coincidences are very strong. One of the most striking things I suppose about your experience – which you refer to as the hours by the window – in solitary confinement – was this feeling that a veil had fallen and that you'd been in touch with what you call the real reality, and you say that you had a great feeling or a direct certainty that a higher order of reality existed. And that it alone invested existence with meaning. Now since then, thirty years have passed. How has this affected your life?

ARTHUR KOESTLER: Well while the experience lasts, you know, it's very intense. You live on a sort of tragic plane –

* Transcript of a discussion with Anthony Grey, from the television programme *One Pair of Eyes*, in which he related his experiences as a prisoner in China, June 26, 1971.

removed from everyday reality, removed from the trivial plane. Then the prison doors open and you are back in reality and the small worries of everyday life. And the intensity of that experience fades. Don't you feel that?

A.G.: Yes, I find that was a compromising situation; one compromised with a fierce ideal.

A.K.: And one even occasionally asked oneself, did I really have that experience? So it's a sort of diminishing-return thing. But on the other hand I think, on a deeper level, it has sort of reorganized your personality. In a less obvious way than –

A.G.: Yes. One of your analogies, which I think is very nice, is the real reality being written in invisible writing, writing which we can never read, which we only intuit by seeing a fragment from time to time. It's like a captain who goes to sea with sealed orders in his pocket, and when he gets to a certain point he opens his sealed order only to find the writing is invisible. But you say nevertheless the fact that he has these orders make him behave differently to a man without them. How has this affected your behaviour or your enjoyment, your appreciation of life? Knowing that you had the orders as it were.

A.K.: Well, I do believe in it. I think it is so, but these are things very difficult to put into words, and I think one shouldn't talk too much about it, you know, because one talks it away.

A.G.: Yes, one of the most striking things you said when I first met you was that some of the things which happen to a man in solitary confinement should perhaps be subject to the Official Secrets Act.

A.K.: Or a private Official Secrets Act.

A.G.: Yes. Why do you say that?

A.K.: Because you talk it away, you change it into small coin, you know.

A.G.: One of the things which I found most comforting in a sense reading some of your writing was that you felt you couldn't verbalize this experience, you couldn't put it into words. And this is what I found when I wrote the closing chapter of my book. I found myself saying, it's beyond words, feeling that I was incompetent or inadequate; that you had also found it was beyond words was very reassuring.

A.K.: Yes, and when you try to put it into words, it becomes either sort of maudlin or it becomes too intellectualized – I mean these are experiences which just resist being put into everyday ordinary language.

A.G.: Do you think that everyone would benefit from a spell of solitary confinement by casting off what you call the layers of irrelevancy?

A.K.: No, I think the opposite. I think it depends on the individual. I have seen the opposite – people becoming nastier, bloodier.

A.G.: There were times when I was alone for two years when I felt grateful for being alone, that I didn't have to share my cell or my room with another prisoner. Did you feel this?

A.K.: I felt it very much so. I have talked to . . . you know, lots of my friends have been through jail in the East, and to my utter surprise some of them say that if I have the choice I would always rather share a cell than be alone, to be alone is unbearable. I could never really put myself, project myself into that kind of mind.

A.G.: I felt that I only had myself to deal with. I felt I could deal with myself, but I couldn't necessarily control somebody else.

A.K.: No, oneself is already a handful, you know, but – (*quiet laughter*)

A.G.: Looking through *Hostage in Peking*, did you feel that there had been similarities in our reactions?

A.K.: Oh very much so, yes.

A.G.: I noticed for example that we both walked up and down – you walked up and down six-and-a-half paces, I walked up and down eight-and-a-half paces.

A.K.: But the question is how wide your stride is.

A.G.: But that you had taken great care to step into the middle of the flagstones and not on the line. If you could do this five times everything would be all right, you would be released. I did a very similar thing.

A.K.: Knowing how stupid it is.

A.G.: Knowing. All the time.

A.K.: And not being able to –

A.G.: Not being able to do anything about it.

A.K.: And accepting it so. Knowing how stupid it is, being helpless against it, then one tells oneself, all right, you are stupid and superstitious, accept that it's part of you. Then it's all right.

A.G.: Yes. This is probably part of the coming to terms with oneself which is a very important aspect of being left alone I think.

A.G.: I also remember very vividly – there was a cat jumped up outside your cell quite often, it couldn't get in because of the wire across the window. You were quite desperate to have the cat inside with you. I think this probably expresses a basic human desire for some kind of comfort or some kind of company.

A.K.: Do you remember *The Birdman of Alcatraz?* In solitary this seems to be an absolutely universal experience, that a bird or a cat or even a spider –

A.G.: In my case ants.

A.K.: In your case ants – becomes sort of out of all proportion important.

A.G.: Yes. I think perhaps this is the thing that tends to emphasize the feeling of a man in solitary confinement, that he is really only an aspect of total reality. Do you not agree?

A.K.: I do agree. And again I find difficulty in putting that into words. It's very intense.

A.G.: The feelings which you seem to develop in what you call the spiritual hothouse, you said solitary confinement is a spiritual hothouse, which I think is a very splendid summing up of it – you developed a feeling, an identity, a sympathy for other people, which you probably hadn't had before, and I think I shared this. This was one of my reactions which I shared with you. And as you said in your autobiography, my seemingly absurd and over-strong preoccupation had, I felt, a desperately direct bearing on the state of our society, and on applied politics. How did you feel about this when you came out? Did you feel it was relevant, because to talk about things in these terms may sound – I feel I sound terribly naïve to those concerned only with the utilitarian realities. Do you feel it's applicable in any way and do you feel it should be applicable?

A.K.: I think it does influence your whole outlook on life, including politics. Because though I haven't been an eye-witness of the execution of my fellow prisoners – but I've been an ear-witness, you know; I heard when the cell doors were opened, when the priest came with his sanctus bell, between twelve and two at night, and then the chap – very often – because they were Spaniards, they shouted, '*Madre, madre,*' mother, you know. They didn't know until the last minute whether the sentence had been confirmed or commuted. Only when at night the cell door was opened by the procession of the warder, the priest, then it was read – the decision was read out to them, that either they are going to go away for thirty years which was of course an absolute bliss – or to be shot within ten minutes, you know, taken out and shot. And then a very – quite a lot lost their nerves. In political theory you talk of the necessity to liquidate hostile elements, to eliminate – these are abstract words. But when you had heard these shouts and they ring in your ear, then you realize that one of the basic tenets of one type of politics, that the end justifies the means, has become unacceptable. You just don't accept any longer, that *any* reason, any superior lofty reason, justifies these acts. And that makes a very fundamental change in your outlook.

A.G.: This is what changed your attitude towards Communism, I assume, is it?

A.K.: I think so. Oh yes ...

A.G.: You also said that this idea of subjugating the individual to an abstract ethic, you said that not only Communism but any political movement which implicitly relies on purely utilitarian ethics must become a victim of the same fatal error. It leads to torture chambers, inquisitions, the guillotine; whether in fact the road is paved with quotations from Rousseau, Marx, Christ or Mohammed, it makes little difference. If there is system, if there is a dogma, if there is a greater body to which the individual should subscribe, in fact it leads to this oppression of the individual.

A.K.: Whatever the abstract idea, the methods become unacceptable.

A.G.: Although the whole outcome of this is difficult to put into words, I was talking to a Chinese friend of mine the other day and he was showing me an old painting in which a very beautiful lotus-flower grows from the mud. And I think perhaps in a sense there is this element of an experience of confinement, imprisonment, in solitary confinement, coming back to normal life and seeing it, at least for me, with a new awareness, a new appreciation of this – something very good and worthwhile coming out of something very bad. Do you agree?

A.K.: I do agree but with an addendum. That you are also all the time aware that in your trivial preoccupations you sort of walk over manholes with horrors underneath, you know. It's both. Both what you say – a more intense enjoyment of existence while it lasts, but at the same time also more intense awareness of what's tucked away under those manholes.

A.G.: Yes. I think you said in one of your chapters that you like to think that the founders of religions, prophets, and so on, had at moments been able to read a fragment of what you call the invisible texts, but they so padded and dramatized it, that they themselves could no longer remember what was authentic about it. I would like to think this too. Do you in fact subscribe to any formalized religion now?

A.K.: No, I do not.

A.G.: Like myself you probably feel the abstract existence of something which is indefinable.

A.K.: Yes, except in symbols which are for me of equal

validity whether it's a cross or the crescent half-moon or the shield of David. They are symbols, man-made symbols for a reality which cannot be formulated.

A.G.: . . . I was talking to a hermit on a small rocky island in the Channel, and I put this question to him. And he said that he felt that people involved in religion in civilized society were simply in it for what they could get out of it. I think that's probably an extreme reaction but I think he had some truth in what he said. He also said he felt there was some force out there on this small barren island in this Channel, he felt there was some force. I think this is a reflection of our kind of conclusions. Perhaps we shouldn't even call them conclusions, it's too hard a word. Just a reflection of the kind of things we feel after being alone.

A.K.: Yes, because you see – I just said that every symbol has for me equal validity. But at the same time those symbols can become very poisonous. Lead to religious wars, inquisition and so on. The danger of overconcretizing an experience which should not be concretized.

A.G.: It seems that we have a desire to oversimplify and hide behind symbols rather than being satisfied with what we're having now, a very inconclusive, a very tenuous and groping discussion about what we feel to be reality.

A.K.: And that symbol is then in danger of becoming a slogan, a totem pole, a war cry.

A.G.: Yes. You said that England with its muddled ways lives closer to the text of the invisible writing than any other country. You said that the English people are suspicious of causes, contemptuous of systems and bored by ideologies and sceptical about Utopias. It's a country of potterers in the garden and stickers in the mud. This is why you chose to live here. Do you still feel this true today?

A.K.: Yes. There are certain inroads, disquieting inroads. But on the whole I think it is so.

A.G.: And also another symptom we seem to share is over-sensitive reactions to other people in our daily lives – to the taxi driver or the charwoman. I find that I react very strongly to a small smile or a shrug or a – an instance of rudeness. Do you still find this thirty years later, do you think that's a continuing thing?

A.K.: Yes. I think one becomes oversensitized, you know. When one's day was made or undone by a warder's smile, by a rudeness or some kind of human kindness, one jumped at it like a dog at a bone, you know. Something to chew on. I think that has given one an allergy against hostility, rudeness and sensitivization towards –

A.G.: I think it takes time to build up a protective shell again. Perhaps one doesn't ever entirely.

A.K.: Up to a point, yes. But one is more sensitive I think.

A.G.: In *Dialogue with Death* you make a mystifying statement; you say, in the Seville death house you paradoxically felt most free. How was that?

A.K.: I think 'freedom' has several meanings. One is simply that you are confined to so much space and there are bars around you . . . Then there is your feeling of inner freedom, of being alone and confronted with ultimate realities instead of with your bank statement. Your bank statement and other trivialities are again a kind of confinement. Not in space but in spiritual space.

A.G.: And why when you were confined to the four walls did you feel most free?

A.K.: Because you are sort of stripped naked, facing ultimate reality, life and death . . .

A.G.: Facing yourself really, do you think?

A.K.: And the universe. So you have got a dialogue with existence. A dialogue with life, a dialogue with death.

A.G.: This is an area which most people don't enter into.

A.K.: No. Well, most people do have a few confrontations in their lives, when they are severely ill or when a parent dies, or when they first fall in love. Then they are transferred from what I call the trivial plane to the tragic or the absolute plane. But it happens only a few times. Whereas in the type of experience which we shared, one has one's nose rubbed into it, for a protracted period.

A.G.: What about when one arrives back on the trivial plane? What do you think are the most threatening things to individual freedom in normal society?

A.K.: To go to the other extremes, suddenly, and to throw away everything and say, oh these were just overwrought nerves and silly thoughts. To diminish and thereby to destroy the genuineness of the experience.

Excursions and Pilgrimages

*The Faceless Continent**

On long-distance flights airlines compete for first-class
passengers with sumptuous menus and little gifts – slippers,
socks, perfume. Qantas, the Australian airline, also had a
surprise in store for us : an S-shaped plastic hook, Woolworth
style, attached to a piece of cardboard which contained the
following printed instructions :

About your Serviette
We have designed your serviette so that you can attach it easily
to the neckline of your clothes. Before fixing it in position, all you
need do is push the narrow end of the clip attached to this card
through the buttonhole which has been made in one of the corners
of the serviette. (See illustrations.) We hope you will find this aid
helpful.

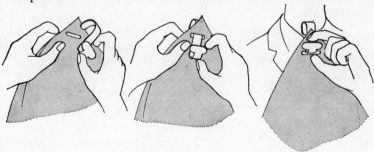

If you wish, you may keep the clip as a small souvenir of your

* First published in the *Sunday Times*, 25 May 1969.

flight with Qantas. You'll find it makes an ideal hanger for clothes when placed at the top of a car window.

I never had a mental image of Australia. With most countries, whether one has been there or not, one tends to associate some picture or symbol, however naïve: geishas for Nippon, bullfighters for Spain, and so on. But Australia was a blank in my mind – kangaroos are not people, and the convict ships are as remote as the Pilgrim Fathers. But that plastic hook, and the napkin with the hole in it, did the trick for me: they became a symbol of something in the Australian character which is both touching and putting off – goodwill devoid of grace, a down-to-earth pragmatism that can be aesthetically offensive, a culture that is deliberately, almost defiantly, suburban.

Australia is a suburban continent. Its cities spread shapelessly like ink on blotting paper, because there is such a vast amount of empty space available. The continent has an area thirty-two times the size of Great Britain, inhabited by less than twelve million people. On the British Isles you have to share a square mile with 500 other people, in Australia with three. Australians have the biggest housing plots *per capita* in the whole world. Melbourne has a quarter of the population of London, but covers an area twice as big, which means that a Melbourne family occupies eight times more living space than a London family.

Seventy to eighty per cent of Australians own their own houses. The average house has more than five rooms, and less than one person to each room. It is a single-floor bungalow, mass-produced in weatherboard, red brick or asbestos cement. It has a front lawn and a small garden, possibly with a couple of gum-trees. It may look shabby or posh according to the suburb in which it stands. 93.5 per cent of the population of Sydney, and 92 per cent of the population of Melbourne, live in suburbs outside the municipal boundaries. To paraphrase Parkinson's Law, cement tends to expand to fill the available space.

If one of the dominant features of Australian life is suburbanization, another is – urbanization. Less than 15 per cent of the population lives in rural areas, and less than 10 per cent are actually engaged in farming. Australians enthuse about the bush, but they live in cities. They are in fact the most highly urbanized nation in the world.

So the continent holds two world records: first, in cramming nearly everybody into the towns; second, in providing them with such lavish amounts of living space per head that the towns keep bursting at the seams and spilling their contents further and further away from the centre into the blue yonder. The first process precipitates urbanization, the second suburbanization; the first concentrates, the second dilutes. If you were to draw the map of Australia in the manner of an astronomical chart, the big towns would not be stars but spiral nebulae.

Needless to say, the gradual shift of people from the centre to the periphery is noticeable in European and American cities, too; but in Australia it has been carried to such extremes that the very concept of the city is beginning to lose its meaning, and 'urban civilization' is replaced by 'suburban civilization'. In Melbourne or Sydney, it may take an hour to get from one's suburb to the centre. As a result, these capital cities, each with a population of well over two million, have no night life – which, after all, is an integral part of urban civilization. 'Kings Cross' – the Piccadilly Circus of Sydney – is long before midnight as dead as an abandoned gold-digger town.

A social survey in a representative suburban housing estate showed that 98 per cent of the residents never went out in the evening except on Saturdays. Eighty-five per cent watched television daily for all or part of the evening – and Australian television has to be seen to be believed. The week we arrived, Mr Arthur Cowan, General Manager of the Federation of Australian Commercial Television Stations, bluntly declared in a speech: 'We know that there is no real demand among viewers for cultural programmes' – by which he meant 'classical music, art and sculpture'. And the Australian writer, Keith Dunstan, reported: 'Five radio stations out of six and three television stations out of four give us nothing but football on Saturdays.'

The survey just quoted included a questionnaire; one of the questions was what the subject would do if he were suddenly given A$10,000 to spend. Only 6 per cent 'mentioned the idea of a trip'. And when housewives were asked what they would do if they had more domestic help, only 17 per cent 'had the idea of going out more'.

Why? The answer is perhaps that in the dreary confines of suburbia there is nowhere to 'go out' except the petrol station. In spite of the immensity of its open spaces and ocean beaches, Australia can give the visitor a feeling of claustrophobia. Or perhaps one should put it the other way round and say that a suburbanized culture tends to be affected by agoraphobia – a fear of the open spaces of the mind. The simplest defence against this danger is conformism, which in the Australian middle classes has been carried to even more stifling extremes than in the United States. By a perverse twist of history these two continents, pioneered by the most adventurous, 'rugged individualists', produced the most philistine societies of our century (with South Africa as a runner-up). And paradoxically, conformism breeds loneliness. The thin-lipped Yes of conformity is not an advanced form of human communication; nor is its loud-mouthed, matey variant. Australian crowds have a smell of loneliness – you can feel it in the bus, in the pub, at the races, on the beach.

So, I am told, has Australian sex. Since I had no firsthand experience of it, I have to quote a social worker, the Reverend Roger Bush, reporting in the *Sydney Sunday Mirror* on 'a problem rife in the tidy wilderness of suburbia'. The problem is wife-swapping. The Reverend describes the case histories of four couples in a suburban neighbourhood, who for six months swapped wives regularly every couple of weeks by drawing lots, until their marriages went to pieces. All four men belonged to 'the white-collar, junior executive classes'. 'They've had no decent form of entertainment available in their own social groups and not been able to afford the long treks to the bright lights for entertainment. They are the victims of the poverty of their own existence in the affluent society . . . I have already counselled the victims of wife-swapping arrangements from seven different Sydney suburbs, and I know of other cases which have occurred in the smaller cities of New South Wales.'

No doubt it will turn out to be a short-lived epidemic like the Hong Kong flu. Another curiosity is the 'hambone' – a male striptease act performed at private parties, and (according to Craig McGregor's excellent *Profile of Australia*) even as a public show at Kings Cross – though I do not know whether it still exists. At the same time, the vice squad wages an all-out war against homosexuality. Judging by official statements, it is a major problem in Australian society – and probably will remain one so long as it remains punishable among consenting adults.

This, roughly, is the superficial and somewhat depressing picture which many visitors form after a few weeks in Australia. But although I believe it to be a truthful picture as far as it goes, it is nevertheless superficial because it fails to take into account the radical change the continent is undergoing. Its effects are as yet scarcely noticeable, but they are bound to transform the Australian profile within the next two or three decades.

The nature of this transformation can be summed up in a few figures. In 1947, when the Australian government embarked on its mass-immigration policy, the country had a population of seven and a half million. In the next twenty years Australia took in more than two million immigrants, only a third of whom were British; two thirds came from the Continent. In 1947, 90 per cent of the population were of British origin. Today the proportion has fallen well below 80 per cent, and in another twenty years it is expected to fall to 60 per cent. In other words, by 1990 four out of every ten Australians will be of Italian, Greek, German, Maltese, Hungarian, Polish or Turkish origin. From an ethnically uniform continent Australia is being rapidly transformed into a cosmopolitan mosaic.

The mass-immigration programme, with a present intake of 150,000 people per year, aims at a population of around thirty million by the end of the century. It is guided by the slogan 'Populate or Perish'. Its psychological origins date back to the early war years when Australians discovered with a shock the vulnerability of their under-populated continent. The invasion of New Guinea brought the Japanese to their doorstep; even more traumatic were the effects of a minor Japanese air attack on Darwin, and the ineffective shelling of Sydney by Japanese submarines. At the Évian Conference on the refugee problem in 1938, Australia refused to take in any German Jews threatened by extermination, with the frank statement: 'As we have no real racial problem, we are not desirous of importing one.' After the war, her attitude changed to the opposite extreme. Australia accepted 170,000 refugees from D.P. camps in Europe, and embarked on a mass campaign to woo immigrants from all over Europe. Even the White Australia policy is no longer enforced quite as rigidly as it used to be; there are some 12,000 young Asians studying at Australian universities, and some 30,000 Asians have become permanent residents or even citizens of the country.

The formidable process of self-transformation in which the continent is engaged raises equally formidable problems. But so far the average Australian seems to be either unaware of them or to ignore them with a shrug. The immigrants keep pouring in; their presence, amounting to one in five, is felt everywhere. The attitude of the true-bred Australian is not hostile; he justs pretends that they are not there, with the slightly embarrassed look people have when travelling with strangers in a lift.

I visited some of the dismal immigrant hostels: Nissen huts in former army camps, where new arrivals are housed until they find more permanent accommodation – which may take anything from six months to two years. These hostels are for the vast majority of immigrants their first experience of their future country, and they come as an ugly shock. Some are well run, others less so, but all have the depressing atmosphere of an army camp. An Australian Senator, J. P. Ormond, denounced them as 'disgusting and degrading'. This is certainly not what the immigrants expected – nor what they were led to expect by the alluring handouts of Australia House.

It could be objected that the families of agricultural labourers from Southern Europe, or of unskilled workers from British industrial slums, had lived in even worse conditions. This may be true, but psychologically even a hovel of one's own may seem preferable to a concentration camp without barbed wire. This comparison is less frivolous than it may seem, because most immigrants on arrival have no alternative but to go to a hostel – and, what is worse, without knowing when they will be able to get out of it.

The cause of this misery is the housing shortage. Only a small percentage succeed in buying a house within the first five years of their arrival. This refers to the lower-income classes among immigrants – but about 90 per cent belong to this category, and less than 10 per cent to the professional and semi-professional classes. A large proportion arrive by 'assisted passages', which means that the fare for adults over nineteen is only about £10 per head, while any amount of children travel free. This means an immense investment on the part of the Australian government, and it is a surprising lack of foresight that no commensurate effort has been made to provide housing for the people they were so anxious to attract.

An interesting sidelight on the reasons why Britons emigrate was recently provided by an opinion poll. Apart from the answers one would expect – general dissatisfaction with conditions at home, hope for material betterment, etc. – one curious factor emerged: the 'last-straw effect'. Families may for several years vaguely talk of emigrating until some trivial grievance – a penny added to the price of beer or a leaking pipe – precipitates the decision. Then they take the plunge, without proper preparations.

Oddly enough, the Italian and Greek immigrants find it generally easier to settle down than the Pommies. They move in with relatives or friends in the Little Italys and other ethnic enclaves in the poorer suburbs; conditions may be cramped, but nevertheless preferable to the Nissen hut, and they can start right away saving up for a house. They are also traditionally more enterprising in various trades, from cafés and grocery shops to market gardening. According to the 1961 census, 20 per cent of Italians and Greeks were employers or self-employers as against 12 per cent of U.K. immigrants (what's happened to the Nation of Shopkeepers?).

On the other hand, these ethnic enclaves have a tendency to turn into ghettoes, with all the ugly possibilities which that implies. The city areas in which they congregate, such as Melbourne's inner suburbs, consist of old, derelict buildings not much better than slums. Many children in the inner suburban schools are unable to speak English well enough to receive proper tuition. The result is, in the words of a teacher, that the child 'leaves school with a smattering of information and a superficial knowledge of English which will probably keep him behind a sales counter for the rest of his life.' Or, alternatively, doing the types of menial chores which true-bred Australians are less and less willing to do.

As for the liberal professions, only British and some American degrees are recognized; doctors, dentists, vets, engineers from the Continent have to follow courses and sit for examinations *after* their arrival, with no certainty that they will pass. Skilled craftsmen are up against the same barriers; most of them are recognized as assistant craftsmen only.

The overall effect of these restrictive provisions is a kind of 'unnatural selection' which works against the badly needed professionals and in favour of unskilled and semi-skilled labourers, who are not always of the most desirable human material. If this policy continues, Australia will soon have a large proletariat of foreign origin superimposed on the suburban idyll. Instead of a melting pot it may become a cauldron.

Thus the 'Populate or Perish' programme is itself beset with perils. To aim at thirty million by the end of the century means to quadruple the population within a span of fifty years – a rather unique experiment even in the age of the population explosion. Taking an optimistic view, some of the difficulties I mentioned may be no more than teething troubles; but the problem of the Australian future goes deeper than that. The search for identity has become a fashionable phrase, but in Australia it is a real problem and a haunting one. It has two related aspects, one internal, the other external.

Looking inward, there is a general uncertainty whether the desirable aim is the melting pot, out of which the third generation of immigrants is supposed to emerge re-cast to fit the Australian way of life – or whether it is preferable to aim at unity-in-diversity, by preserving the cultural identity of the various groups in the ethnic mosaic. And should the mosaic include Asians – such as Hong Kong Chinese and Fiji Indians? The American and Canadian precedents are much discussed, but are more confusing than helpful.

Turning to the world outside, the question arises whether Australia is an Asian country – and if not, what else? Nominally, Australians are still 'British subjects', although the Government is bringing in legislation to alter their status to 'Australian Citizen and British Subject'. But as *The Bulletin* wrote recently, 'What does British subject mean? The answer is – nothing at all. We are not subjects of Great

Britain. We do not share either the duties or the privileges of the people of that kingdom.'

However, to Australians this is not a question of international law, or even of national pride, but of security and survival. Another leading Melbourne paper wrote: 'The old certainties have begun to dissolve, and Australia is now being swept swiftly and erratically towards an Asia in which the domination of Western power can no longer be taken for granted. The final retreat has sounded for Britain's garrison forces in Malaysia and Singapore, and the British Fleet, for generations the guardian of Australia's aimless isolation, is sailing for home. A new hesitancy now runs through American policy . . . Australia can no longer trust its security and its survival to the presumed patronage of powerful friends . . . Australia must now dare to stand with and by its nearest Asian and Pacific neighbours.'

That sounds nice, but how can you become an Asian country if you discriminate against Asian immigrants? On that question the paper remains silent, and the politicians remain silent, although to a large extent the problem of Australian identity hinges on it. In an age of increasing racial and ethnic tensions it is a terrifying decision to make – and it can only be made by the Australians themselves; all pious liberal advice from outsiders tends to oversimplify the problem and to ignore the bitter realities of group psychology. One cannot help but sympathise with the predicament of a nation which, descended from truculent forebears, tried to cultivate peacefully its little gardens on an inhospitable continent, and to create a suburban idyll in an unidyllic age.

Farewell to Gauguin

A Joyless Traveller's Guide to the South Pacific*

How our friends envied us . . . The poor things had just started scanning the annual holiday supplements to discover how to make their travel allowances work the miracle of the loaves and fishes, while we were setting out on a round-the-world tour via Persia to Australia and back through the South Pacific and Caribbean. An enterprising Australian television company paid for the round trip – first-class air fare, first-class hotels, including the wife. How everybody envied us!

The journey took two months, and we returned, to coin a phrase, impoverished by the experience. Looking back at it, much of it seems like a journey through an air-conditioned, neon-lit tunnel, filled with the ubiquitous sound of muzak, the smell of hamburgers, and the sight of blue-haired matrons spending the life insurance money of their deceased husbands on package tours from one duty-free shop to the next. Every day about 5.30 P.M., the tunnel changes into the dark womb of the same cocktail bar in the same Hilton or Sheraton in Honolulu, Fiji or Teheran; and subsequently into the same Rainbow Oak Room, where the same freeze-broiled choice

* First published in the *Sunday Times*, 13 April 1969.

T-bone is banged down by the same Italian waiter beside the same spluttering fancy candle on your table. Never a native dish. Never a tropical fruit. And all the time, day by day in every way, the muddy floods of muzak pour down on you, piped into the lift, the lobby, the loo, bar, restaurant, swimming pool, coral beach – a tonal diarrhoea, unrelenting, inescapable. There are world-wide crusades for the preservation of wildlife and countryside; it is time somebody started a movement for the preservation of silence.

The explosion of the tourist industry, and its culture-eroding fall-out, are still regarded as a minor nuisance. It is more than that. All over the world the tourist trade is an increasingly important factor in the national economy. In some countries it takes first or second place, and in some the number of tourists per annum outnumbers the total native population. It is a plague of locusts which brings to the natives material prosperity and cultural corruption, eroding traditional ways of living, contaminating arts and crafts with the vulgarity of the souvenir industry, and levelling down indigenous cultures to a uniform, mechanized, stereotyped norm.

It is a global phenomenon. In the alpine meadows, the farmers are turning into innkeepers; tourists are easier to milk than cows. If French gastronomy is now hardly more than a legend revived each year by new editions of the *Guide Michelin*, it is an indirect consequence of the explosion; why should the chef waste hours on a dish when the customer from overseas drenches it in ketchup, and the natives soon learn to imitate him? One has watched the blight spread over Europe, from the gulf of Naples to the Swedish fjords; but I still had some illusions left about the Pacific islands, the 'palm-fringed jewels of the sea', as the travel brochures invariably describe them, 'where all of life sways to music and every heart responds to gaiety and laughter'.

The first of the jewel islands we descended on, on our way back from Australia, was Fiji (more precisely Viti

174

Levu, the central island of the group), which may serve as a fair sample. All the old hands in Sydney had told us that it was less spoilt than Noumea or Tahiti or Hawaii, and up to a point this seemed to be true. I must confess that I also had a naïve curiosity about the place because, according to the reports of nineteenth-century missionaries and anthropologists, the 'Feegeeans' were by far the most cruel and savage people among the Pacific islanders – and the most prodigious man-eaters, who practised cannibalism on an unprecedented scale, partly as a ritual, mainly because of a genuine addiction to human flesh. One Methodist missionary, the Reverend John Watsford, reported in 1846: '. . . The poor wretches [captives of a hostile tribe] were bound ready for the ovens, and their enemies were waiting anxiously to devour them. They did not club them lest any of their blood should be lost. Some, however, could not wait until the ovens were sufficiently heated, but pulled the ears off the wretched creatures and ate them raw . . .' The last case of cannibalism is supposed to have occurred some thirty or forty years ago – nobody is quite sure – in a village a few miles from Nadi International Airport, and there are rumours about more recent cases in the interior. I mention this to indicate that cannibalism is not merely a subject for funny *New Yorker* cartoons, but a tradition that has survived within the span of living memory in Fiji; perhaps the starkest symbol of the abyss that separated one type of human culture from another only two or three generations ago. So one could not help wondering whether any traces of a mentality beyond our imagination could still be discerned by the perceptive eye.

The perceptive eye's first discovery at Nadi Airport was a tourist leaflet which had a map, a list of the various duty-free liquor allowances for travellers to the United States, Australia, Noumea, Tahiti, Mexico, and so on; and also a list of 'helpful words and phrases in Fijian'. The complete list of helpful phrases (omitting the translation in Fijian) ran as follows: 'Go away.' 'I am broke.' 'Another round.'

'This is lousy.' 'Where is the entertainment tonight?' 'Take me to the Skylodge.' 'Girls, stop crowding me.' 'Have we met before?' 'I am very romantic.' 'You are an extremely attractive young woman.' 'Take me to your chief, leader, etc.' 'Where is the manager?' 'You are standing on my foot.' 'My friend needs a doctor.' 'Driver, take me home.'

To make my point clear: nobody in his right senses could wish to go back to the world of the head-hunting cannibal. But nobody in his right senses can rejoice to see it succeeded by a trashy tourist's paradise surrounded by native slums. Yet this is what has happened to Fiji and the other islands. Some years ago, Alan Moorehead wrote:

> In Tahiti the Polynesians had been taught to despise their own religion and had torn down their temples. In the same way, the Australian aboriginals' gods and totems had been brought into contempt by the white man and had been destroyed and forgotten. This left the natives without a tradition or a past, and they were like men who had lost their memories; they walked about in a trance in the materialistic present, and they could not be anchored to the new white god. Backwards as well as forwards the way was blocked.

The quote is from Moorehead's book, *The Fatal Impact: An Account of the Invasion of the South Pacific 1767–1840*. Since then the Pacific, and vast areas in the rest of the world, have suffered a second fatal impact. The first was colonization; the second one might call coca-colonization. The first destroyed the fabric of existing cultures without providing a replacement; the second enveloped them in a plastic pseudoculture, expanding like a giant bubble-gum. The first imposed itself by rape, the second by seduction. But seduction of a victim under the age of consent is considered a crime, whether the victim is a person or a culture.

If Europe also shows signs of becoming coca-colonized, it has only itself to blame – its lack of vitality and decline of self-confidence. Even so, the process here is gradual and partial, and there is a strong, healthy resistance against it. In Melanesia or Polynesia, Hawaii or the Caribbean, the impact is more brutal and appalling because there is no resistance rooted in living tradition; it is an explosion in a vacuum. Farewell, Gauguin.

The first impact wrought havoc through syphilis, booze and the destruction of social cohesion. The second impact works through industrialization, the mass media and the tourist trade. A fortnight before we got to Nadi, the kingdom of Tonga was gripped by oil fever. A certain George Faleafa, while digging a well, had struck black, oily stuff; within a fortnight, Mr E. G. Wallace, Executive Vice-President of the Republic Mineral Corporation of Texas, was on the spot to confirm the find, and the *Tongan Chronicle*'s headlines screamed: 'Nukualofa is Sitting on Top of Oil for Miles – Samples Same as Texas Oil – This is the Real McCoy!' The King of Tonga was quick to point out that the Republic Mineral Corporation of Texas was not the only one interested in doing a deal; while the Corporation expressed its intention 'to probe for oil in other Pacific areas and Fiji in particular'.

There was also excitement in Samoa, where an Australian real-estate tycoon announced his intention of moving in and 'getting things really going' – by building more super de luxe hotels. In the meantime, the Fijians themselves were busy with their eighth Annual Tourist Convention, which voiced enthusiastic predictions of 'further tourist explosions in the early 1970s when we expect four times as many visitors as at present. They will be travelling in parties of up to two hundred.' The Chief Minister, Mr Ratu Mara, referred to tourists as 'manna from the sky and sea', and stressed the importance of ensuring that this 'manna had the widest possible distribution'. He also sounded a cautious warning to the effect that the impact of the tourist industry on 'what was largely a coconut cash subsistence economy was forcing the Fijians to be jacks of all trades and masters of none'.

In fact they do not become jacks of all trades – which would not be so bad – but underpaid and mostly untrained

M

workers of the catering industry: waiters, cleaners, 'boys', barmen, doormen. They are a magnificent race: mostly six-footers with statuesque figures, a successful cross-breed of the Polynesian conquerors and the older Melanesian stock, with the black, crinkly hair and dark skin of the latter and the sensitive, quasi-European features of the former, which make them look at the same time ferocious and gentle. They smile and laugh readily, perhaps all too readily, whenever they catch your eye; it has become almost a reflex. One cannot help suspecting that in a race where tribal war was chronic, the ritual laugh conveyed the same message as the outstretched hand with the open palm: see, I carry no weapon, nor evil intent.

To watch these athletic great-grandsons of cannibals at work serving dinner to the tourist mob is quite a study. Some of them are tip-hunters and sycophants of the same type as elsewhere; the others, who have preserved their dignity, are polite and withdrawn, laugh less often, and seem rather absentminded. When irritated or out of their depth – which happens frequently, as they understand only a few words of English – they have an odd way of fidgeting and doing a rhythmic tap dance with their fingers; office girls when annoyed engage in the same display on their desk. It is a shared peculiarity – we called it the Fiji fidgets – which seems to indicate a chronic malaise. But late in the evening, when muzak yielded to a native orchestra, playing a characteristic Fijian rhythm with an abrupt stop between two bars, all the waiters fell to filling the gap by banging on bottles and glasses, bamboo screens, windows and table-tops, anything within reach. It was a joyous outburst, a spontaneous breakthrough of compulsive rhythmic motion, which seems to be always latent in their bodies, so that they fall into dance steps under any pretext – even the charlady carrying a bucket along the corridor.

This may be the reason why the South Sea Islanders have gained the reputation of being such a happy lot of carefree hedonists. In fact, rhythmic motion is simply second nature to them. Their only form of music is drumming, stamping and beating sticks together; but that does not necessarily express a carefree disposition, as so many romantic observers thought. Rhythm may express desire in a love dance, fury in a war dance – but also frantic irritation at having to perform the crazy rituals of arranging and changing knives, forks and napkins, emptying ashtrays non-stop, filling up glasses, and listening to incomprehensible orders relating to an incomprehensible ceremony. One particularly fidgety giant forgot the first four courses of our six-course menu, and roared with laughter once he saw that we thought it funny. Another one stood glued to my elbow, and after each sip filled up our wine glasses to spilling level. When I told him not to bother, he said very quietly, 'But this is what I am paid for.' He had been a waiter for seven years, and now earned £4 10s a week, out of which he tried to save £1. Before becoming a waiter he had wanted to be a mechanic, but could not get on with the Indian garage-owner.

This leads to the main problem of the island which, as one might guess, is a problem of race. Fiji became a British Crown Colony by the Act of Cessation in 1874. Soon afterwards the colonial administration began importing indentured labourers from India to work on the sugar plantations. The Indians multiplied. In 1884, there were 3,000 of them, fifty years later 83,000, another thirty years later nearly a quarter of a million. They had become the majority, outnumbering the Fijians at the rate of five to four; and they have taken over the commerce, business and transport of the island. All the shops are Indian (selling mostly duty-free cameras and transistor radios); so are the garages, taxi companies, sight-seeing tours. There is not a single Fijian in trade on the whole island. The vast majority keep to their villages (rows of neat, widely spaced houses with a framework of timber covered with lattice and bark, thatched roofs, artful lashings instead of nails, and coloured prints of the British Royal Family over the bed). The only alternative is menial work and the catering industry; and most of them – including our wine waiter – plan to go back to their villages after they have saved a little money.

Needless to say, the Indians are a hard-working and industrious lot; and they are hated by the Fijians, as all hard-working and industrious strangers are who try to monopolize trade – whether Armenian, Greek, Parsee, Jew or Chinese. There is virtually no contact between the two races, and so far only sporadic violence – the Fijian villagers getting increasingly fond of throwing stones at passing Indian cars. There are only about 10,000 Europeans (a term which includes Australians) living on the island; the British administration does its decent, unimaginative best, mainly relying on the restraining influence of the village chieftains, whose power is still the main social factor in Fijian life. They know on which side their bread is buttered, and have a vested interest in keeping things quiet. What is going to happen when the next generation of more educated and less docile chiefs take over is yet another question-mark to be pinned on the global map bristling with question-marks. One answer was given by a quiet Australian engineer who lives in Fiji: 'I only hope I will no longer be here at the time.'

One thing is certain: for the British to clear out completely and wash their hands would lead to catastrophe. The white man's burden has come back with a vengeance (but who was responsible for shipping Negroes to the Caribbean and Indians to Fiji?). Perhaps the Australians, who have large capital investments on the island, may be persuaded to take over one day; but they show more enthusiasm for building lucrative tourist hotels on the Coral Coast 'where every heart responds to gaiety and laughter' than for shouldering new responsibilities.

Thus Fiji provides another illustration of the distressing paradox of our time – that the world is rapidly moving towards a mass-produced, uniform culture, and yet at the same time both the global confrontations and the venomous local conflicts of religion, language and race are getting not less but more acute.

Of course there were 'bright intervals' on the journey, as the weatherman is wont to say. The palms are there, swaying in the breeze, the coral reefs and the mangrove forests; and if you get up a couple of hours before the package awakes, you can even enjoy a swim. But the grim question-marks are also there, as they are in every part of the world through which the tourist caravan-trail passes. The majority, however, travel like registered parcels, unaware of the natives, their aspirations, problems and tragedies. Instead of promoting mutual understanding, they promote mutual contempt. Like an ocean liner leaving a trail of pollution, they leave a trail of corruption in their wake.

The main responsibility lies with the organizers – the robber barons of the travelling industry, who, instead of providing information and guidance for their charges, treat them like a bunch of battery-reared hens, expected to lay three golden eggs per day. But to paraphrase an old saying: tourists get the package they deserve. Perhaps a one-year world tourist strike would decelerate the explosion and improve matters. Otherwise we shall soon have muzak on the moon, with weightless spaceburgers.

In the meantime, let us stop dreaming of lonely beaches and native dishes in the South Seas. The big hotels do not serve them, and in most places there is nowhere else to eat. Nor can you get papayas, mangoes or other tropical fruit, although the trees outside are heavy with them: they are too much bother to handle. The only approved shape for fruit is a neat cylindrical tin; it is always just ripe and need not be peeled. If you want exotic food, go to an exotic little restaurant in London; if you hanker after tropical fruit, go to Fortnum and Mason; and if you want to know what a trip around the world is like, spend an hour in the Hilton. It is cheaper than a package tour, and you do not have to ask on your return that soul-searching question on wartime posters:

'Was your journey really necessary?'

Marrakech*

To turn a cliché into a paradox, Marrakech is where the Arabian Nights survive at 8 degrees longitude west of Greenwich. As one habitually associates Islam with the East, there seems to be something bizarre about minarets out-flanking church spires. Stranger still, the founders of this African city were, and the majority of its inhabitants still are, a white race – the enigmatic Berbers.

Marrakech is a Berber city: its character and atmosphere still betray its origin as a nomad encampment, market centre, permanent funfair and super-brothel for the men from the Atlas and the Sahara. The Berbers are highlanders and desert people, converted to Islam in the eighth century. As the Celtic inhabitants of Britain succeeded in preserving their ethnic identity in the mountainous parts and regions of difficult access, while in the fertile plains it became diluted by successive invaders, so the Berbers preserved their tribal structure and ways of life in their own backwoods of sand and snow. But Marrakech, unlike other Moroccan cities, never lost out to the late-comers – whether Arabs, Negroes or French. Although situated in the balmy plains, it belongs to the Atlas, whose white ghost peaks are omnipresent above its red walls and palm groves; and it belongs to the Sahara, whose emissaries – camels, Blue People, Tuaregs and other

* First published in the *Sunday Telegraph Magazine*, 8 September 1972.

dusty nomads – are as much in view and at home in its souks as farmers in their Sunday best on market day in Tewkesbury. In short, it is not so much a city as an oasis; of the desert, though not in it.

Like the Basques and some other Celtic–Iberian people, the Berbers are a puzzle to anthropologists. They called themselves the Sons of Shadow and the Daughters of the Night. According to one theory, they migrated in prehistoric days from Spain to Africa. Their language is said to be related to Welsh, and their blood-group ratios are said to resemble that of the Basques. But they could also be descended from the Phoenicians; or the Canaanites driven from Palestine by Joshua's trumpets; or from one of the Lost Tribes. Could be, maybe, perhaps. All that seems certain is that they are not of African origin, that their appearance is often more nordic than that of some Latin people, and that they are remarkably good-looking. A considerable proportion are descendants of mixed Negro–Berber ancestry with darker skin and curly hair, but they do not have either flattened noses or fleshy lips; the gene for the hawk-like profile appears to be dominant. The most famous and influential Berber was, ironically, St Augustine, promoter of the papacy.

They are often mistakenly thought to be Arabs because their language is written in Arabic script. In antiquity, they had a script of their own, but they somehow lost it – except the Tuaregs, who still carve the same angular characters on Sahara rocks which are found at archaeological sites on the North African coast dating 2,000 years back. To complicate matters for the traveller, there are large Jewish communities who speak Berber, and Negro communities – mostly former slaves – who do likewise; while the educated Berber prefers Arabic, which is the official language.

The red walls of Marrakech first appeared among the palm groves in 1062 around a fortified nomad camp, raised by

Yussef ben Tachfin. His tribe of veiled camel-riders and horsemen from the South Sahara called itself Al Marabitoun, 'the frontier warriors of the Faith' (hence *Marabout*, holy man), but Spanish historians melodiously corrupted this into Almoravides. Yussef ben Tachfin was a warrior saint who lived to the age of ninety-six and brought the whole of Morocco under his control. He undertook several expeditions into Spain, defeated the army of Alfonso VI near Badajoz, then deposed the various effete Arab princes, took possession of Granada and gained mastery of all Moslem Spain. Under the dynasty of the Almoravides, which he founded, the Berber empire reached its first peak; within the lifetime of a single generation, the mud walls of the former nomad encampment grew into the ramparts of its imperial capital. Yussef himself assumed the title 'Emir of the Moslems' – which was only a hair's-width from the Caliph's title 'Emir of the Faithful'. Thus Marrakech became the Baghdad of the West, rivalling Harun al-Rashid's city in splendour and corruption. But whereas Baghdad's glory has been erased by Mongols, Turkomans and progressive city-planners, under the red walls of Marrakech one can still dream oneself back into the past over a cup of mint tea and a whiff of Kif.

If the frequent mention of red seems repetitive, it cannot be helped. It is the first breath-catching impression one gains as the plane approaches the town, and it lingers on when one has left it, as a nostalgic desire to go back for more. The city lies in a fertile plain called Blad el-Hamra, 'The Red', dotted with palm groves, olive groves, citrus groves and fruit-trees of all descriptions as far as the foothills of the Atlas, only fifteen miles away. The plain is covered by a net of irrigation channels lined with cactus hedges or eucalyptus – a kind of liquid lacework. In the midst of this African Eden the massive ramparts rise abruptly into the sky, enclosing the city in a zigzag line like an angular doodle some ten miles in circumference, pierced by ten splendidly arched and sculpted gates. The wall is built of *tabiye*, the red earth of the plain, which was once baked in the sun, then in kilns, and is now mixed with stone and rammed into concrete blocks. Parts of it are crumbling, others have been patched up or rebuilt heaven knows how often, but it makes no difference, because the material used is still the same, the contours of the majestic doodle are still those which ben Tachfin's tribesmen drew around their camp, and its colour is still the same – except that it is never the same colour. For it changes hourly, from rose-pink to orange to carmine to terracotta, according to the state of the sky and the time of day. The overall impact is not of permanence in frozen time but of timelessness and gentle decay. The walls are crumbling like trees shedding their leaves.

The modern quarters, built outside the walls at the time of the French protectorate, are surprisingly in keeping with the character of the rest. When one has witnessed the rape of old cities all over the globe, this almost seems a miracle. The French planners appear to have fallen under the spell of the place; they used the same red building-materials, rectangular designs, pure cubes, Mauresque arches, slim pillars and capriccio turrets for their public buildings as you find in an ancient mosque in the medina, or a kasbah perched on the slopes of the Atlas; even the villas in the residential suburbs all strike the same harmonious chord. There are spacious straight alleys lined with palm trees – the Avenue Mohammed V, Marrakech's Champs-Elysées, is over two miles long; they intersect in roundabouts graced by fountains and not yet disgraced by traffic jams. How long this blissful state will last is another question; already one or two of the new building-sites induce goosepimples even under the African sun. But for the time being the trinity of colours – blue (sky), green (palms), red (walls) – still dominate the scene. The air makes one feel as if one is sitting under a hair-dryer, but it carries an intimation of the Atlas snows and a sprinkling of dust which smells of *khamoun*, the Berber's favourite spice. No wonder there are hordes of hippies around, spotty and fey, living, it seems, on their old-age pensions.

There are few architectural monuments. The successive dynasties who ruled the city were as lavish in building as they were thorough in demolishing what their predecessors had built. The Eiffel Tower of Marrakech is the minaret of the Koutoubia which, as every street-urchin will tell you, is 221 feet high and has three huge brass balls on its top which are said to have once been of solid gold. But in spite of its fame it leaves one rather cold. It was built – by Christian slaves – under the reign of the Almohades, who replaced the Almoravides, on the ruins of the huge castle which the Almoravides erected and the Almohades destroyed.

The rulers were both aesthetes and vandals, savage and refined. The most heartbreaking testimony of grandeur and decline is the Palais el-Bedi. It was built by Ahmed el-Mansour, 'The Golden', and pulled down a century later by Moulay Ibrahim, Morocco's 'Sun King'. Ahmed, a contemporary of Queen Elizabeth, conquered the Sudan and brought back huge quantities of gold and slaves; both were put to use in erecting el-Bedi, 'The Marvel'. Only the walls are left to testify to the vast dimensions of the palace; they form a kind of rose-coloured labyrinth round an inner patio, the size of a parade ground, where once hundreds of horsemen performed their fantasias. The Marvel has vanished, but one fraction of it is preserved; the pavilions, or mausoleums, containing the royal tombs of the Saadi dynasty. The Saadis were the only Arab dynasty which ruled Morocco (in the sixteenth century), claiming descent from the Prophet's son-in-law; even Moulay, the 'Sun King', in his jealous rage did not dare to destroy their tombs. He merely walled them in, blocking all access, and so they stayed for more than two centuries, until 1917, when the French cut a narrow passage into the wall, a kind of hidden backdoor to the holy of holies.

Unbelievers are not allowed to enter the pavilions, but can feast their eyes through the open archways. They are jewels of Islamic architecture. In each of the pavilions the high vaulted ceiling is supported by marble pillars, while the walls and the ceiling itself are dazzling, glittering expanses of faience, mosaic, carved cedar, carved stone, gold inlay, filigree, all traceries and arabesques. It reminds one of microscope photographs of the structure of complex crystals, where geometry turns into poetry, symmetry into music. It is a perverse thought that these and other wonders of Islamic decorative architecture, from India to Spain, were inspired by a censorship of unique rigour: 'thou shalt not make unto thee any graven image or any likeness of anything . . .' Christianity took the Second Commandment metaphorically, orthodox Islam literally. Not permitted to represent life, the creative urge exploded in an orgy of abstract arabesques and cascades of colour.

The actual tombs, in the centre of this kaleidoscopic exuberance, are austere slabs of Carrara marble cut to size – short for the royal children, longer for the parents. The marble was, according to the guide, paid kilo for kilo in sugar or spices. The carved inscriptions on the tombs are quotations from the Koran, and contain no reference to the manner of death of the occupants, which almost without exception was violent and nasty; Abdullah the Golden poisoned by one of his sons, Abd el-Malek stabbed to death by his bodyguards, El Abbas killed by his uncles, Abdul Abbas and his children murdered by the governor.

But worse was to come – in the shape of Moulay Ibrahim, whom historians like to call the African 'Sun King', but whom his contemporaries called The Bloodthirsty. This remarkable character had 2,000 wives in his harem, who bore him 800 sons and, presumably, as many daughters. (The figures were reported by a British Embassy led by Commodore Stewart in 1721.) He also kept a menagerie of lions, tigers and leopards, fed mostly on slaves. He was kind to animals; his camels were shampooed three times a week and his pet dogs lived on strips of delicate flesh sliced from the buttocks of his women. He did worse things than that; but we had better remember that he was just a little lamb compared to the Führer. The barbarities of the Moors revolt us because they seem arbitrary and wanton, whereas our own obey an impeccable logic.

One of the Moulay's famed acrobatic stunts was to mount a horse and with a stroke of his sword sever the head of the servant who held the stirrup, all in a single, graceful move. On a similarly aesthetic impulse, he demolished the royal palace in Marrakech and built his own Versailles in Meknès, which became the new capital. From that event dates Marrakech's decline. Officially it remained one of Morocco's four imperial cities, but the seat of power alternated between Meknès, Fez and Rabat, and the successors of Moulay Ibrahim (the Alouite dynasty, still reigning) only sojourned occasionally in Marrakech. Their local palace, the Bahia, built at the end of the nineteenth century, is a non-sight with furnishings inspired by Early Woolworth.

The power and the glory have departed, but local colour and tradition have been preserved, and life for the humble people of the souks is relaxed and timeless. Marrakech is still the playground of the Atlas and the Sahara. The centre of attractions is a huge, dusty, octopus-shaped square, the size of several soccer-fields, the famous Djemaa el-Fna. The name means Parade of the Dead, because in bygone days rebels and criminals used to be decapitated, and their pickled heads displayed on poles around the square.

The Djemaa el-Fna is the greatest tourist attraction in West Africa, but the vast majority of tourists are still, as they were in the days of the original nomad encampment, tribesmen, shepherds, peasants and craftsmen from the deserts and mountains of the interior. They come on donkeys, bicycles and archaic buses, wrapped in burnous or djelaba, to sell their wares – anything from dates to camels and carpets – and to enjoy the sights of the permanent funfair of the Djemaa. But they do it in a quiet and dreamy way; they form circles around a story-teller, snake-charmer, letter-writer, horoscope-caster, mime or musician, then drift on to the next attraction. Always round any performer there is an inner circle, mostly of children and oldsters, squatting on the earth, and a more volatile outer perimeter, equally silent, never pushing or craning. On the roof-terrace of one of the cafés overlooking the Djemaa one can play the ant game: pick out one brown-hooded figure among all the other brown-hooded figures and try to follow its slow, apparently aimless zigzag course among the stalls and circular crowd formations. But it is not easy to keep track of one's ant; the most successful record was (each move taking about five minutes): negotiates with sweetmeat vendor, buys one – watches monkey performing – listens to Koran preacher – buys coconut, which vanishes inside burnous – listens to story-teller – negotiates with Berber herbalist, but does not buy – watches black dancers – gets lost from sight; end of documentary.

The Djemaa has the magic of a revolving stage. In the morning it is an open-air market. At midday, it is dotted with food-stalls which sell delicious charcoal kebab, beautifully arranged bowls of couscous, flat loaves of unleavened bread, fruit, sweets. In the afternoon, the funfair. When darkness falls, the food-stalls again, lit by candles or kerosene lamps, in a white cloud of kitchen fumes. At night, a desert oasis, with huddled figures everywhere, sleeping in the dust.

If the Djemaa has the shape of an octopus, its tentacles are the souks. Miles of them. Labyrinthine, claustrophobic miles of smells, colours, din, jostling by donkeys, bicycles, Vespas, tip-carts. I have lived for nearly four years in the Middle East, but I have never understood what the souks live on. A dozen nut-stalls in a row, mountains of millions of nuts, all of the same varieties, all interchangeable. Tens of thousands of babouches, leather belts, Atlas rugs, trinkets, miles of dyed fabrics, tons of joss-sticks and spices. Who is to buy all this? There is perpetual motion and chatter, but one rarely sees actual business being transacted, money changing hands. The souk is not an occupation but a way of life. It is the women who do the real work, in the fields and in the towns. The men used to be busy waging tribal wars, now they smoke, gossip and drink mint tea. Does one approve or disapprove? Let the behavioural scientists work it out.

But there can be no doubt about one's attitude to the Berber women. The first time we drove up into the Atlas we thought it was some national carnival day. How else could one explain the sight of a girl labouring in a field with a hoe *in a dress of gold lamé*? But they are all decked out on all days in the most flamboyant colours, gaudy but beautifully matched, and adorned with silver necklaces and baubles, whether walking to their village with pitchers on their heads or bundles of faggots on their backs, or hacking away with their hoes in a grove or on the narrow ledges of a terraced mountain. The hoes, unchanged since the pharaohs' artists drew them, shine like old silver when not in actual use; polishing them must be a cult. They are peasant women of Berberic splendour, who return your admiring stare with bold smiles which seem like invitations; yet I have never seen one walking or talking with a man.

To feel the pulse of Marrakech one has to explore its surroundings, the villages and kasbahs which provide its influx of people and goods and maintain the continuity of custom and tradition. 'Kasbah' signifies stronghold; it may mean anything from a castle to a fortified village or walled-in dwelling. Driving up into the High Atlas and down again towards the Sahara, you find kasbahs in the most unlikely places, perched on the rocky mountain-side or tucked into arid valleys, all but invisible at first, because they are built from the mud and stone of their surroundings, hugging the slopes out of which they were carved and into which they dissolve by a kind of architectural mimicry – villages like chameleons. The walls look blind and forbidding, with small square holes for windows, the roofs are flat, overgrown with grass; many are deserted, walls crumbling, dust returning to the earth as it was. But even when inhabited, there are few signs of life: some elders by the roadside, sipping their eternal tea like the Danaïdes condemned to drawing water through a sieve forever; some asses braying, or one of the female peacocks languidly returning from work. And as a backdrop, the eternal white peaks swimming incongruously in the blue blaze.

Principal feature of the local news from Marrakech in *Le Petit Marocain*:

Sensational Finale of the Wild Boar Shooting Season

Last Sunday was the last day of the boar-shooting season. A team composed of some of the most distinguished guns of our town produced a sensational bag. By sensational we mean that one of the trophies was a white boar. A boar devoid of bristles and with a white skin. This 'albino' of a new kind was three years old, weighed eighty kilos and was as fat as a sow.

This is a rare event and our friends have tried to establish the animal's pedigree. Some of them think that the explanation is quite simple.

A wild sow in an amorous mood apparently permitted herself one day to be seduced by a common domestic pig. She must have made a reconnaissance in a pig-sty on a farm and accepted the advances of a partner, who thus begot a boar of a new variety, which, in spite of its white colour, lived with the wild herd until last Sunday, when M. Nanoud Agouram felled it with his gun . . .

There followed the list of all successful and unsuccessful hunters, both Arab and French.

Other local news items during our sojourn: Annual Meeting of the Atlas Trout Association to hear the secretary's *Rapport moral et financier*. In the Centre Culturel Français: films by Jean Cocteau, readings from Malraux on the philosophy of action. Royal Automobile Club of Morocco: Bridge Tournament. Gala dinner of the Association of Corsicans in Marrakech, attended by 150 guests. Annual Meeting of Association of Bretons in Marrakech re-elects President. The Parents' Association of the Lycée Victor Hugo dissolved because of lack of interest on the part of parents.

Highlights on the telly: readings from the Koran, news in

Arabic, news in French, seventh episode in the serial 'The Sevilla Fan'.

There are only a few thousand Frenchmen left in Marrakech. These and the rich Arab families form the upper crust. They keep to themselves – trout-fishing, boar-hunting, looking at Cocteau films. They may occasionally be seen in the international luxury hotels, but never in the old town, not even in the cafés and *brasseries* of the new town. The fight for independence ended fifteen years ago; the remaining, invisible Frenchmen are being eased out of their remaining jobs; there is no tension, but there is a feeling – like the tender spot left by a recently healed wound . . .

My bumper clicked against the bumper of a local citizen's car. There was no visible damage on either side, but the citizen tried to persuade me that his right front mudguard had come loose. He drummed a tattoo on his right mudguard – it made a sinister hollow sound. I drummed a tattoo on his left mudguard – it made the same sinister hollow sound. A young Berber policeman stood by and made soothing noises at him. In the end the citizen gave up, but he had the last word: *'Ca va – mais seulement pour te montrer que nous n'sommes pas des vâches – nous sommes pas des sauvages!'* (The endearing *tu* is the only address in Moroccan French.)

Des sauvages they certainly are no longer. The danger they are running seems to be rather of the opposite kind, of increasing numbers becoming parasites of the tourist invasion. Particularly the children, who swarm round the visitor like gadflies, with an insistence I have not encountered even in India, offering themselves as guides, touts, Lolitas of both sexes.

This phenomenon is something quite different from the classic, institutionalized forms of prostitution in Morocco and some other Islamic countries, where sex was always regarded as a precious gift of Allah, which should be enjoyed as such, in gratitude to Him. The brothels were the poor man's harems, which enabled him to partake of that gift. To be a prostitute was neither shameful nor dishonourable.

A man entering her room was supposed to exclaim 'I am God's guest'; and as if to confirm this, pious prostitutes had the first line of the Koran tattooed on the depilated pubis. Most women of the Berber tribes had a chain tattooed instead, as a protection against the evil eye – but perhaps also as a symbolic chastity belt.

Marrakech, the trading centre and playground of the Sahara, had one of the most picturesque red-light districts in the world; it was one of its principal industries. Its Pashas used to pay their armies with their revenues from prostitution which was taxed like any other trade. The French troops stationed in Marrakech added to the boom; when the brothels were finally abolished in 1955 by the present Sultan, there were 27,000 officially registered prostitutes in the town, which had a total population of 240,000. A little arithmetic yields the astonishing result that over 10 per cent of the total population; i.e., 20 per cent of the female population; i.e., 40 per cent of all females of child-bearing age, exercised that profession.

And now? There are probably just as many of them – but without registration, protection, medical supervision, social status. Perhaps Gresham's Law applies also to mores. And one is left wondering what course European history would have followed had Christianity subscribed to the belief that liquor is an invention of Satan, sex a gift of God. In Marrakech, it sounds plausible.

The Glorious and Bloody Game

In the summer of 1972 the *Sunday Times* invited me to write about the chess world championship match between Boris Spassky of Russia, the title-holder, and Robert (Bobby) Fischer of the United States, the challenger. The first article that follows was written before the match (which took place in Reykjavik, Iceland); the second during and after the match.

I. REFLECTIONS OF AN ADDICT*

So here we are all agog to watch this bizarre bullfight where nobody knows which is the matador and which the bull.

This is yet the kindest metaphor we can apply to the contest. The 'we' refers to an endearing fraternity of men, to which I am proud to belong, known as the Passionate Duffers. We worship Caissa, the Muse of Chess, but owing to the inadequacy of our mental equipment can never hope to attain to her favours, condemned as we are to remain lifelong amateurs in the double meaning of that word: dilettantes and *aficionados*. Thus protected from the temptations of the arena, we have remained pure at heart and are all the more distressed by the degrading antics displayed prior to the match by the contestants and their *banderilleros* in the Russian and American Chess Federations. The haggling about the

* First published in the *Sunday Times*, 2 July 1972.

195

venue and the revenue, the political invectives and insinuations, made one almost feel that chess is a game too noble to be left to the chess-players.

Yet – except for the added spice of another East–West confrontation – there is nothing new in these unsavoury proceedings; there have been other greedy *enfants terribles* before Bobby and other smug dogs in the manger before Spassky among the masters of the past; and champions such as Lasker, Capablanca, Alekhine behaved just as badly before they played the immortal games which we play over and over again like our favourite recordings of Beethoven quartets – some of these recorded games date back indeed to Beethoven's days.

Edward Lasker (namesake of the great Emanuel, and himself a grand master) wrote a revealing book with the title: *Chess for Fun and Chess for Blood*. But 'fun' is the wrong word; what he meant was that the game of chess is the perfect paradigm for both the glory and the bloodiness of the human mind. On the one hand, an exercise in pure imagination happily married to logic, staged as a ballet of symbolic figures on a mosaic of sixty-four squares; on the other hand, a gladiatorial contest. This dichotomy is perhaps the main secret of the game's astonishingly long history – dating back at least a thousand years – as a favourite pastime of princes; of its insidious addictiveness and the symbolism of the chess-board as a microcosm. It is reflected in a celebrated passage in T. H. Huxley's *Lay Sermons*:

> The chess-board is the world; the pieces are the phenomena of the universe; the rules of the game are what we call the laws of Nature. The player on the other side is hidden from us.

There's the rub – if only he were hidden, a disembodied spirit, instead of being out for your blood, blowing cigar-smoke into your eyes, humming snatches from the *March of the Toreadors*, or commenting on each move with a quotation from the Bard – like that character in Lasker's book who, when attacking a piece, would say: 'Get thee gone, Mortimer, get thee gone!', and when his own queen was attacked would squeal: 'Why appear you with this ridiculous boldness before My lady?' In my own chess days in the Café Central in Vienna I was driven mad by another character who, each time he gave check, would whisper insinuatingly *Schachutzi mit dem Putzi* . . . If you don't get the meaning, you save a blush.

Such are the dismal mannerisms of duffers, but our revered masters are not above more sophisticated psychological warfare tactics. The two classic chess instruction books of the sixteenth century were written by a Spaniard, Ruy Lopez, and a Frenchman, Damiano. Both recommend in dead earnest that the hopeful student should always place the board in such a way that the light, of sun or lamp, should shine into the opponent's eye. And in his world championship match against the title-holder, Steinitz, Lasker asked to be seated at a separate table because old Steinitz sipped his lemonade with a loud noise (the umpire refused the request). No wonder that Bobby Fischer fusses about lighting, seating arrangements, hotel accommodation and other trivia. 'The Russians cheat at chess to keep the world title,' he was reported to have said. 'They have tried by every means to avoid me. They also slandered my name. They are afraid of me. They have been putting up road blocks for me for years . . .' And about the forthcoming match: 'It will probably be the great sports event in history. Bigger even than the Frazier–Ali fight. It is really the free world against the lying, cheating, hypocritical Russians.' Bobby is a genius, but as a propagandist for the free world he is rather counterproductive.

Spassky struck a milder note. He did not accuse Bobby of lying and cheating, only of suffering from persecution mania. Bobby boasted that he would 'trounce' the reigning champion. Spassky retorted with a modesty gambit: he was not sure of the outcome, but in case victory went to Bobby, 'I should be the happiest man alive if I were no longer champion.' That explains perhaps why for the last six months he submitted to a gruelling physical and mental training for the match, running several miles a day and studying the records of all the important games that his opponent had played in the past. Bobby did the same.

Both are wonderfully cast for their roles; Fischer the rugged individualist, adventurous and occasionally reckless both in his life-style and chess-style; Spassky the more benign type of Soviet bureaucrat, cautious, non-committal, evasive. For the last twenty-four years the world championship has remained a Russian monopoly, jealously guarded, carefully fostered by state grants, *datchas* and other privileges for the masters. Never in all these years has a Western challenger had a better chance of bringing back the ashes across the Iron Curtain. Accordingly, the Reykjavik contest has been dubbed 'the match of the century' before it has even started; and the unedifying prelude was quite in keeping with the emotional issues involved.

Murder in the cathedral

Yet, all personal, political and tribal passions apart, the bloodiness would still be inherent in the royal game, and if it were not there the game would not be what I called it before – a symbol or paradigm of the working of the human mind. Chess is a battle of ideas; and the most savage battles have always been fought for ideas. No wonder that Caissa emerges from the medieval twilight with a tantalizing smile and a dagger in her hand. She haunts oriental legends and nordic sagas in dramatic episodes where princes stake their fortunes or realms on a match against an outsider – who infallibly wins and is infallibly slain for his pains.

Tradition has it that the game originated in the first millennium in India when the Buddhist influence was still predominant; and since Buddhists reject violence, they invented chess as a substitute for war. Firdousi relates how it was imported from India into Persia, where the Arab conquerors adopted it and eventually passed it on to Europe. Harun al-Rashid, Charlemagne and Canute are all alleged to have been passionate duffers, who got involved in violent chess incidents; but it is, oddly enough, in the great Icelandic sagas that Caissa stands revealed as a real bitch. The Icelanders were devoted to her – and obviously still are; a sixteenth-century traveller, the Norwegian priest Peder Clausson Friis, reported that the Icelanders 'especially occupied themselves with the practice of the game of chess, which they play in such a masterly and perfect way that they sometimes spend some weeks' time – playing each day – on a single game, before they can bring it to an end by the victory of the one or the other combatant'.

In contrast to these peaceful marathons in more or less civilized times, the chess episodes in the sagas relate to games which were short and violent, preceded by boasts and ending in slaughter. My favourite yarn is in *St Olafs Saga*, where King Canute plays a game with Ulf Jarl (Earl Ulf). Canute blunders, making a hasty move which makes him lose a knight; then, in true duffer style, recalls his move and makes another instead. Ulf is furious, upsets the board, and takes sanctuary in a church – where he is slain the next day by Canute's henchmen.

Thus Reykjavik is not such an odd venue for the great event as it might seem to those ignoramuses who have not read the scholarly and voluminous work *Chess in Iceland and in Icelandic Literature* by Williard Fiske (published, in Florence, by the Florentine Typographical Society in 1905, with a memorable index of thirty-four pages).

One might think that the game owed its popularity in these extreme latitudes to the long polar nights which did not favour outdoor sports. But Cuba has a tropical climate, and yet Havana, at the end of the last century, was the Mecca of chess, where several world championships were played and where the native world champion, Capablanca, was worshipped by the whole country. Persia, Iceland, Cuba and the Soviet empire became addicted at different periods, regardless of climate and race, as if by the spreading of an epidemic carried by strange bugs – twice six different types of pieces on a simple chequered board.

But why all the nastiness, why the apparent malignancy? The reason is intuitively felt by every chess-player, yet difficult to explain without giving the impression of indulging in artificial profundities. In the first place, each chessman, whether bishop, rook, knight or queen, embodies a dynamic threat, as if it were alive and animated by the desire to inflict the maximum damage (by attack or defence) on the opponent's men. When a chess-player looks at the board, he does not see a static mosaic, a 'still-life', but a magnetic field of forces, charged with energy – as Faraday saw the stresses surrounding magnets and currents as curves in space, or as Van Gogh saw vortices in the skies of Provence. Thus there is a strong element of animism and magic in the game. Lewis Carroll was aware of it when he chose chessmen as the dramatis personae for *Through the Looking Glass*; and the Red Queen's 'Off with his head' could come straight out of an Icelandic saga. I cannot refrain from quoting here some lines from a poem by the seventeenth-century pioneer of Sanscrit studies, High Court Judge and poetaster, Sir William Jones – because in its touchingly naïve manner it conveys the mythological flavour of the game:

> *The champions burn'd their rivals to assail,*
> *Twice eight in black, twice eight in milkwhite mail;*
> *In shape and station different, as in name,*
> *Their motions various, nor their power the same . . .*
>
> *High in the midst the revered king appears*
> *And o'er the rest his pearly scepter rears . . .*
> *On him the glory of the day depends,*
> *He once imprison'd, all the conflict ends.*
>
> *The queens exulting near their consorts stand;*
> *Each bears a deadly falchion in her hand;*

Now here, now there, they bound with furious pride,
And thin the trembling ranks from side to side . . .

Behold, four archers, eager to advance,
Send the light reed, and rush with a sidelong glance . . .
Then four bold knights for courage fam'd and speed,
Each knight exalted on a prancing steed . . .
Four solemn elephants the sides defend;
Beneath the load of ponderous towers they bend.

Now swell th' embattled troops with hostile rage,
And clang their shields, impatient to engage . . .

When the battle is over, there is a tragic finale:

Now flies the monarch of the sable shield,
His legions vanquish'd, o'er the lonely field . . .
He hears, where'er he moves, the dreadful sound;
Check *the deep vales, and* Check *the woods rebound.*
No place remains: he sees the certain fate,
And yields his throne to ruin, and Checkmate.

Echoes of Lear on the lonely heath – 'blow winds and crack your cheeks! rage! blow!'

And rage they do. For, after all, the little buggers on the board, however alive they may seem, including the revered king and his queen of furious pride, are master-minded by one's own mighty brain. In playing bridge or poker or scrabble, there is a large element of chance which provides a convenient excuse for being beaten. In chess, there is no such excuse. And the worst misfortunes are those for which one has oneself, and only oneself, to blame. It might seem that similar considerations apply to tennis or boxing, where also skill, not chance, decides the issue; and some of the stars in these games do indeed take defeats hard. But even if one is in principle prepared to put physical skill on a par with mental aptitude, the mind itself which makes these judgements won't have any of it. To be called clumsy is an acceptable insult; to be called stupid is unpardonable. The great Alekhine, when beaten, often threw his king across the room, and after one important lost game smashed up the furniture in his hotel suite. Steinitz, on a similar occasion, vanished from his quarters and was found disconsolately sitting on a bench in a deserted park. He died insane. So did Morphy, who preceded him as world champion. Morphy suffered from persecution mania; Steinitz from delusions; he thought he could speak over the telephone without using the instrument and that he could move chessmen by electricity discharged from the tips of his fingers. What sane person could devise a symbol more apt for the omnipotence of mind?

In the weeks to come we shall have the opportunity of watching two men facing each other in silence across the high-voltage board, where every move could make the fuses blow, each in a kind of waking trance, making the figures perform an imaginary dance which exists only in their mind's eye, then mentally rearranging them in a different configuration, and yet another one, variation upon variation, while the ballet-master himself remains immobile and the kaleidoscopic changes of scenery all take place inside his skull.

While the game is on, it is only the choreography that matters – aggression is sublimated into dazzling acrobatics. There may be more unedifying episodes to come, but whatever happens, the fraternity of Passionate Duffers craves your indulgence for the magicians of the glorious and bloody game. . .

2. A REQUIEM FOR REYKJAVIK*

In the prehistoric days before the great match started, I wrote in these columns: 'Chess is a game too noble to be left to the chess-players.' The scandalous preliminaries seemed to confirm this with a vengeance. But I also made the optimistic forecast that once the match got under way, it would produce

* First published in the *Sunday Times*, 3 September 1972 (the match ended on 31 August).

some immortal games which we shall replay in years to come like our favourite gramophone records. Whether they were immortal or not, we must leave to posterity to decide; but to humble amateurs at least most of the twenty-one games played will remain a moveable feast. Some carry distinctly Wagnerian echoes – young Siegfried, the kosher hero from Brooklyn, ritually slaughtering the Russian dragon. Spassky's slow, protracted agony evoked the strains of Chopin's Funeral March, while the comedy of errors which ended in the draw of the seventh game was like a duet from an *opéra bouffe* – until the gramophone-needle got stuck in Bobby's perpetual check. The affinities of chess and music have long been recognized; the Argentine grandmaster Najdorf compared Bobby's lovely sixth game to a Mozart symphony.

The overture, however, was an ignoble cacophony, and some of its episodes are worth recalling before they vanish into the prehistoric mist.

The champion arrived in Iceland well ahead of the scheduled start of the match, took up residence at the Saga Hotel and went into training. An empty suite at the Loft-leidir Hotel, at the other end of the town, was waiting for the challenger. The days passed by, but we waited in vain. During the week preceding D-day – Saturday, 1 July – Bobby Fischer three times booked his air-passage from New York to Iceland and each time cancelled it.

Came Saturday, the Holy Sabbath, on which no member of the Church of God – the fundamentalist sect to which Bobby converted from orthodox Judaism – is allowed to travel. The opening ceremony in the national theatre took place in Fischer's absence. The front rows, reserved for the Diplomatic Corps and other dignitaries, were mostly empty. The President of the Republic – a nice, youngish archaeologist – and his pretty lady arrived half an hour late; perhaps they had been praying for a miracle. The proverbially imperturbable Spassky sat in the front row, displaying his imperturbability. The three anthems were duly played and the speeches duly delivered. The Soviet Ambassador spoke grimly of chess as a bridge of friendship between nations. The American Chargé d'Affaires, perhaps more aptly, invoked the episode in *St Olaf's Saga* in which King Canute has Earl Ulf slain because of a quarrel across the chess-board. The gentlemen of the press were debating within themselves whether to describe the event as Hamlet without the Prince or a *corrida* without the matador. The grey day faded into the white night in an atmosphere of subdued hysteria.

Came Sunday. The first game of the match of the century was due to start at 5 P.M. The last direct flight of the day from New York landed at Reykjavik airport in the early morning. No Bobby. I noted in my diary:

Waiting for Godot. Rumours in the Loftleidir lobby: he will arrive on a special plane with Norman Mailer, chartered by Time-Life Inc. (The Time-Life crew, about a dozen scruffy characters, keep acting mysteriously.) He will be dropped by parachute. My own suggestion: he will arrive, dressed as Lohengrin, riding on a swan. Funny to be a war correspondent again after all these years. Everybody's favourite pastime: to psycho-analyse Bobby. Got so bored that slunk away to souvenir shop, bought ashtray made of Icelandic lava, guaranteed to give owner magic powers of seduction.

On Monday we were still waiting for Godot.

Then came Mr Slater's dramatic message to Bobby: 'Come on out, chicken', combined with his offer to double the prize money – and the next day at 6.55 A.M. Bobby erupted from his plane like a rocket, brushed aside the reception committee, ran to his waiting Mercedes car and vanished from sight.

The drawing-of-lots ceremony to decide who should have first move in the first game was scheduled for the afternoon. Spassky was there, Bobby was not. Spassky walked out, after protesting that he had never agreed to the postponement. Dr Euwe, President of the International Chess Federation, commented: 'He gave the impression of having to wait for orders from Moscow.' His guess proved to be correct, for the next development was a cable in broken English from the Russian Chess Federation requesting that Fischer should be 'punished for his behaviour' and that both he and Euwe should apologize. By punishment they meant that Fischer should forfeit the first game through his absence.

At this junction, our Bobby performed an amazing *volte face*. He wrote an abject apology to Spassky 'for my disrespectful behaviour in not attending the opening ceremony. I simply became carried away by my petty dispute over money. I have offended you and your country, the Soviet Union, where chess has a prestigious position . . . I know you to be a sportsman and a gentleman . . .' – and so on. A few months earlier he had called the Russian masters a 'lying, cheating, hypocritical lot'.

However, by eating humble pie he had reversed the situation. If the Russian insisted on the punishment he would be branded as a Shylock. There were more negotiations, more postponements, more hysterics in the wings. Bobby was given his Icelandic *datcha*, his bowling-alley, indoor tennis-court, the use of a 1972 Mercedes in place of the previous 1971 vintage, and his favourite swivel chair was flown in from New York. On Tuesday, 11 July – ten days behind schedule – the first game of the match finally got under way.

It was the most colossal anti-climax of the most colossal match of our colossal times. For the first twenty-eight moves both players indulged in a cautious, colourless game, apparently aiming at a quick draw. Then on his twenty-ninth move, Bobby committed a colossal blunder, sending his bishop straight into the valley of death. When the game was adjourned, Bobby was doomed. When it was resumed the next day, he staged a half-hour walkout in protest against the unseemly behaviour of a cameraman who had poked his head through a vent in the ceiling. When he was persuaded to return to the board Spassky took thirty minutes to finish him off.

Had not young Fischer boasted that he would not lose a single game of the match? Now Nemesis was triumphing over hubris – or so it looked. It looked even more so when at the second game Bobby once again failed to turn up, because of the television cameras. This time he was declared, without further ado, to have forfeited the game. The score now was Spassky 2, Fischer 0 – the champion had secured, rather painlessly, one sixth of the points he needed to remain champion (twelve points out of twenty-four games). Fischer booked airtickets to New York for the following day. He cancelled them when the arbiter agreed that the next game should be played in a secluded private room.

And then, miraculously, Phoenix rose from the ashes. In the third game Fischer got his claws into Spassky right from the opening and tore him to pieces in forty moves.

This game, and the subsequent fourth, taken together constitute the psychological turning-point of the match. In the fourth – which was drawn – Fischer had manœuvred himself into a hair-raisingly dangerous position, but handled it with so much sang-froid and ingenuity that Spassky was unable to drive his advantage home. This seemed to demoralize him even more than his previous defeat. He was still a point ahead, but he was visibly succumbing to the 'Fischereffect' – the myth of Bobby's invincibility. He lost the fifth, sixth and eighth games, and managed to draw the seventh only because Fischer, in a won position, became overconfident and, as one grandmaster commented, 'went to sleep on the job'.

By now, one third through the match, Fischer was leading five points to three. Spassky asked for a two-day postponement of the ninth game for reasons of health – a well-known symptom of demoralization in match-play.

The ninth game was a quick draw, giving both players a breathing-space; the tenth was another brilliant win by Fischer. He now had a three-point lead and the experts predicted Spassky's impending collapse. He was saved, once more, by Bobby's over-confidence, which led to the ignominious loss of his queen, and the eleventh game. The shock had a sobering effect on Fischer, and at the same time revived Spassky's fighting spirit. Not even the loss of the next-but-one game, which restored Fischer's decisive three-point lead, could subdue him. Thus in the third and last phase of the match, games 14 to 21, the world watched Spassky valiantly, and often brilliantly, continuing to fight the lost battle by ceaseless, sometimes reckless attacks; and a chastened Fischer, confident but no longer over-confident, defending his safe lead – not, by any means, through stone-walling tactics, but by rather willingly accepting draws which in the past he would have contemptuously refused. The result was an unprecedented series – games 14 to 20 – of hard-fought draws, of constant thrust and parry, which was even more exciting and entertaining than the wins. The end came not with a bang but a whimper. The twenty-first game was adjourned; when it was to be resumed, Spassky did not turn up but telephoned his resignation. When all is said, it *was* perhaps the match of the century.

As I have said, our main pastime during those early days in Reykjavik was to psychoanalyse Bobby *in absentia*. Since then even people who cannot tell a knight from a bishop have been indulging in that sport. Bobby's dark, intent features were portrayed on the front pages of *Time* and *Newsweek*; there was a sudden boom in the sale of chess-sets and of the records of a 'Viva Bobby' song; his popularity rating was said to be approaching Mick Jagger's. He certainly put chess on the map as it had never been since the days of The Turk – the chess-playing automaton who became the craze of the royal courts of Europe and beat Napoleon (who was a Patzer anyway).

Now the secret of The Turk was that he had someone hidden inside him. But what kind of secret personality is hidden inside Bobby the Tartar? Spassky said he was suf-fering from persecution mania; others that he had megalo-mania; that he had never grown out of being a boy-wonder; or that he was just simply mad as all geniuses are supposed to be. I gladly agree that there is some truth in all these explanations, but I prefer my own, which is simpler; Bobby is a mimophant. A mimophant is a hybrid species; a cross between a mimosa and an elephant. A member of this species is sensitive like a mimosa where his own feelings are concerned and thick-skinned like an elephant trampling over the feelings of others. All of us have met individuals of mimophantic dispositions, but Bobby is the perfect representative of the species. His vulnerability is genuine. The cameras do upset him. He cannot bear street noises. The chair on which he sits while playing, the size of the board grate on his mimosaeque sensitivities. At the same time his elephantine skin prevents him from realizing what he does to others. 'I like to see them squirm,' he commented on his opponents. 'I can see their ego crumbling.' And his favourite comments on his own moves are 'a smash', 'a crunch', 'a chop'.

There have been some half-baked speculations about Bobby hypnotizing his opponents into making inferior moves. There may be a grain of truth in this, if the word 'hypnotize' is used as a metaphor in inverted commas. The best forwards in soccer games seem sometimes 'hypnotized' by a brilliant goalkeeper making apparently impossible saves – as Bobby did in the seemingly hopeless situation in the fourth game of the match – with the result that the attackers shoot either wide off the mark or straight into the goalkeeper's hands. Bobby's opponents in earlier matches seem to have done just that, and Spassky, too, fell under the spell.

For nearly a decade now, the majority of experts have recognized Fischer as the strongest chess-player alive; and his spectacular victories in the quarter- and semi-finals convinced even the remaining doubters. He has the highest tournament rating of any living player on the World Chess Federation's scale, and the highest rating of any player living or dead on the United States Federation's scale. Thus in a way he was justified in regarding himself *de facto* the reigning champion, and his match with Spassky as a mere formality, or even a favour he was doing the title-holder.

Accordingly, it was for him, Bobby, to dictate the conditions. This attitude, based partly on fantasy, partly on fact, was rudely shaken when old Boris unexpectedly staged a counter-walkout, threatened to call the match off and snatch away the crown which Bobby already felt sitting on his head. It must have been a nasty shock for him to realize that he had gone too far; and the rebound, as it were, carried him to the opposite extreme – the grovelling apology to Spassky and the Russian chess world.

Poor Bobby. He does not drink, does not read, takes no interest in women, or music, or nature. He lives in hotel rooms out of two large plastic suitcases. A reporter once asked him what chess really meant to him. His reply was: 'Everything.'

Only one writer could have invented him: Franz Kafka. Spassky, on the other hand, could be the hero of any Stalin Prize-winning novelist. When I try to recall his face I see a kind of identikit drawing, not a portrait. In the Soviet Union, a chess-master is a V.I.P., and a world champion is of course a V.V.V.I.P. His public statements were understandably cautious though often rather whimsical. He pretended to play chess mainly for fun; before the match he told correspondents that he was 'looking forward to Reykjavik as if it were a holiday'. But on a less guarded occasion he made a wry remark to the effect that he did not know what would happen to his much-envied flat in a modern block in Moscow if he lost.

One suddenly remembered that when Mark Taimonov lost his match 6–0 to Fischer, he was deprived of his grand-master's pension. Poor Bobby? Poor Boris. One wonders who is more to be pitied; a state-owned gladiator or a freelance samurai.

Minds and Computers

Now that the match is over and the chess world has sunk into a kind of post-coital tristesse, the non-playing public is beginning to wonder, rather sheepishly, what the whole excitement had been about, and how they had become infected by it – after all, it's only a game, at best a stimulating distraction, at worst a waste of time.

But is it? /

On an earlier occasion I called chess a paradigm or symbol of the working of the human mind. This may have sounded like romantic gushings, but I was in fact expressing a view shared by those scientists who, over the last twenty years, have been busy developing electronic chess computer programs for rather esoteric reasons of their own. The first paper on the subject, by Claude Shannon, a pioneer of modern information theory, appeared in the *Philosophical Magazine* in 1950, under the title 'Programming a Computer for Playing Chess'. His work was taken up by a leading mathematical logician, A. M. Turing, and subsequently by various research teams at Los Alamos, the Carnegie Mellon University, and at the European Atomic Commission (Euratom), headed by Dr Euwe. Each of these groups represented a mixed team of psychologists, mathematicians, chess experts and specialists in that new branch of science known as 'artificially simulated intelligence'. Their purpose was not to build an electronic Turk to beat Fischer and Spassky; they used chess as a means to an end – or, in Euwe's words,

as a concrete representation of human problem-solving and decision-making. If we could design a successful chess-machine, we might be able to penetrate into the innermost of man's intellectual capacities.

The same conviction is reflected in the recently published monumental book *Human Problem-Solving* by Newell and Simon of the Carnegie group. It has 900 solid pages, one third of which are devoted to an analysis of the chess mind. Even more surprising are Euratom's reasons for embarking on such a project. As an international body, Euratom's work is hampered by the difficulty of translating technical papers into a dozen or so other European languages. In the absence of a long-overdue scientific esperanto – the Middle Ages were more progressive in this respect; they had Latin – the obvious answer would be an electronic translating machine. But so far all attempts to build such a machine have proved grossly inadequate. Euratom's chess-research group was guided by the idea that certain analogies existed between chess and linguistics; both have fixed rules or 'grammars' which, however, permit a great variety of choices between combinations of 'moves' or 'words'; and to quote Euwe again, 'in both cases the problem is to limit the choice between many possibilities in an intelligent way'.

The project turned out a failure; and it seems that even the most sophisticated computer chess programs are leading into a cul-de-sac. Yet an experiment with negative results can be scientifically as important as a successful one. Louis Pasteur's failure to demonstrate the 'spontaneous generation of life' out of inanimate substances was a crucial step forward in modern biology; and the apparent impossibility to construct a computer which simulates the processes in the mind of the human chess-player might turn out to be just as important for psychology.

Naïve chess-players occasionally have Walter Mitty dreams of carrying a computer in their brains which will calculate with lightning speed all potential variations ahead of any given position and select each time the perfect move by eliminating, one by one, all the inferior moves. A single example will show that this is impossible. The average number of legally permissible moves in a given position is around thirty. Say it is white's turn to move; to each of his thirty potential moves black has thirty potential answers, which leads, in round figures, to 1000 variations at the end of each 'complete move' (one by white and one by black). Every one of these variations branches again into 1000 sub-variations two complete moves ahead, making a total of a 1,000,000 positions; three complete moves ahead there will be a 1,000,000,000 of them and so on, each move increasing the variations by a factor of 1000. The average length of a game between evenly matched partners of average strength is forty to forty-five complete moves; but, taking duffers into account, it may be a modest twenty-five. Thus in order to decide on the perfect opening move, the Walter Mitty computer would have to calculate at least twenty-five moves ahead (and against a strong opponent perhaps twice as many). To quote Edward Lasker, who is both an International Master and an electronics engineer:

Calculating twenty-five moves ahead would mean that the machine would have to generate a total number of moves in the order of 10^{75} (1 and 75 zeros). Even if the computer could operate at the rate of 1,000,000 moves every second, which is about 500 times faster than the most optimistic program-designer would consider feasible, it would take 10^{69} seconds to complete the calculation.

Well, we couldn't wait that long. Ever since our planetary system came into being, some $4\frac{1}{2}$ billion years ago, no more than 10^{18} seconds have elapsed.

In other words, to compute the perfect move based on the method of elimination known as trial and error (or hit and miss) is not only practically, but also theoretically, impossible. Thus the computer theorist can at least prove that the chess-player does not reason in this way. Now to the layman this seems to be self-evident; he knows intuitively that men, and even animals, do not make decisions by exploring all possible actions in a given situation, including the most absurd or suicidal ones, and ticking them off in succession, until only one course of action is left. But what is self-evident to the layman is not at all so to the psychologist; and for about half a century academic psychology was by and large divided into two camps: the behaviourists, who maintained that the acquisition of knowledge was primarily based on trial and error, and their opponents (the Gestalt psychologists and their successors) who stressed learning-by-insight, that is, by perceiving the essential configurational pattern of a situation as a whole and not as a mere sum of isolated parts. This is an over-simplified account, but it will do for our purpose.

To this controversy (and its wider philosophical implications) the chess computer researchers provided important contributions. They were quick to realize and to prove that to build a machine relying entirely on blind trial and error – exploring all the consequences of all possible moves – was even theoretically impossible. Thus they had to restrict their programmes from considering all permissible moves to a much narrower range of 'plausible' or 'promising' moves; and similarly to confine the analysis of the variations to which these might lead to only two or three complete moves ahead.

But how is the computer to decide which moves are 'plausible' or 'promising'? The human chess-player does it literally 'at a glance'. Experiments of the Euwe team showed that players of master strength needed only five seconds to grasp and memorize the positions of the up to thirty-two chessmen distributed over sixty-four squares. They also studied the eye-movements of the players and found that instead of scanning the board in a systematic way (as, for instance, a television camera rapidly scans a scene line by line), the players' eyes jumped from one strategically focal point on the board to the next in an irregular fashion; in this way he was gaining an insight into the dynamic configurational pattern of the total situation, instead of adding up bit by bit. Instead of considering all moves permitted by the rules, i.e. about thirty, the human player normally considers only three or four 'promising' moves; instead of analysing each into its ultimate consequences, he normally only considers variations two or three moves ahead.

The word 'normally' refers here to relatively quiet situations on the board, where the moves are guided by strategical considerations aimed at improving the player's general position ('positional play') with no dramatic developments in immediate sight. This is the case in the majority of situations in modern chess. In contrast to this are the 'combinatorial' phases of the game where a player pursues an immediate concrete goal aimed at material gain or storming the defences of the opponent's king. In these decisive stages the choice of moves is even more restricted, both for the attacker and his opponent, but at the same time the player considering a risky combination must look much further – sometimes up to ten moves ahead – to decide whether to embark on it. At this juncture he does indeed resort to the trial-and-error method – but of a highly sophisticated kind; he has formed a concrete hypothesis of a complex line of attack and is mentally trying out whether it would end in a hit or miss.

The Carnegie group has shown that a computer can be programed to work out quite clever mating-combinations – precisely because in such situations the choice of the initial move is so narrow that its ramifications can be followed to their final consequences. But the crucial question remains how in normal, 'positional' play the computer should select the two or three 'promising' moves. When a human player is asked why he considers a certain move 'promising', he will reply by some general consideration such as 'consolidating the position', or 'exerting pressure on the opponent', or because the situation reminded him of similar ones encountered in the past – or simply 'because it looks a good move'. But these criteria are too vague and subjective for computer-programing. Thus the researchers had to devise a variety of much simpler 'goals' or 'targets' which would guide the pre-selection of promising moves; such programed targets are: 'material gain', 'increased mobility', 'defence of the king', 'occupation of centre squares' and a few more. But some of these targets may be in *conflict* with each other; thus a player may sacrifice material to get at the opponent's king. To get around this difficulty, the programers assigned a scale of positive and negative numerical values – like school marks – to each 'target'; the aggregate sum of these values for a proposed move is then regarded as a measure of its promisingness. But this crude arithmetical calculation is like a caricature of the qualitative consideration in human decision-making which take the whole situation into account instead of mechanically totting up the size of its various features.

Euwe summed up the lessons of the Euratom project by a frank admission: 'The majority of the research group finally came to the conclusion that this field is much more complicated than was previously supposed and that a breakthrough would certainly not come within a hundred years' – a cautious way of saying never. And he also explained why: 'It is remarkable that the more technical advances we made in improving the chess program the further away we drifted from the ways of human thinking in general.'

Thus it transpires that the machine does not really 'simulate' or reproduce processes in the human mind, any more than the motions of a marionette pulled by strings reproduce the processes of muscle-contractions; man and machine function according to different principles.

There are many reasons why this should be so, apart from those already mentioned. One is that the human player is often guided, sometimes subconsciously, by the accumulated memories of similar situations encountered in the past; but although the computer also has a memory of stored data, it is unable to select and manipulate them in a way even remotely resembling the human way of learning from experience.

But the simplest reason for the inferiority of the computer is perhaps that chess is as much an art as a science. The machine must laboriously compute a move which seems to promise some material gain – but at the price of upsetting more general strategic considerations which are 'above its head'; the experienced player, playing a 'blitz-game' with only three seconds allowed for a move, takes the total situation in at a glance. Picasso's dictum '*Je ne cherche pas, je trouve*' – 'I do not search, I find' – applies to him too.

Blindfold Brilliance

On 9 May 1783 a London newspaper carried the following sensational report:

Yesterday, at the Chess-club in St. James's street, Mr PHILIDOR [a famous eighteenth-century player] performed one of those wonderful exhibitions for which he is so much celebrated. He played at the same time three different games, without seeing either of the tables. His opponents were Count BRUHL, Mr BOWDLER, and Mr MASERES. To those who understand chess, this exertion of Mr PHILIDOR's abilities, must appear one of the greatest of which the human memory is susceptible . . . Mr PHILIDOR sits with his back to the tables, and some gentleman present, who takes his part, informs him of the move of his antagonist, and then, by his direction, plays his pieces.

'Blindfold chess', as it is called, is yet another challenge with which the chess mind confronts the psychologist, and which still waits for an explanation. To play a single game blindfold moderately well is within the capacity of every strong player. To play *three* blindfold games simultaneously was regarded by Philidor's contemporaries as 'one of the greatest exertions of which the human memory is capable'. But in the years that have elapsed since Philidor's day, the record for simultaneous blindfold games has increased by jumps to ten, twenty, thirty-two (Alekhine in 1933); forty (Najdorf in 1943); and on 13 December 1960, at the Fairmont Hotel in San Francisco, the Belgian Master Koltanovski achieved the incredible feat of taking on simultaneously fifty-six opponents blindfold, winning fifty of the games, drawing six and losing none – in an exhibition lasting nine hours and forty-five minutes.

The only remotely comparable achievements that come to mind are those of a few calculating prodigies. But these are rare, whereas among chess-masters the capacity of playing blindfold several games simultaneously is quite common. No systematic study of the phenomenon has been undertaken so far. Alekhine alleged that he could conjure up and 'see' every one of the thirty-two boards as its number was called out – but Alekhine was a notorious liar. Euwe believes that it is not so much a matter of 'seeing' the boards as of memorizing the moves of each game – substituting a story for a photograph – and for that purpose various mnemonic tricks can be used. Yet even so the mystery remains, pointing to vast untapped faculties of the human mind, potentially many times as powerful as those which we put to use in our everyday routines. A thorough psychological study of the mental processes of simultaneous blindfold players might be at least as rewarding as the analyses of the electroencephalographs of meditating yogis.

When all is said, the Russians may not be so wrong in including chess in the school curriculum and treating their champions as favourite pets. Which leaves one wondering how much longer we shall have to wait until the first British master of the royal game will join the ranks of eminent footballers, racing jockeys and cricketers by having a knighthood graciously bestowed on him.

Mahatma Gandhi – Yogi and Commissar
A Re-valuation

Mahatma Gandhi –
Yogi and Commissar
A Re-valuation*

'It takes a great deal of money to keep Bapu living in poverty . . .'[1] Bapu means 'father' in Gujerati, and was used all over India as a title of respect and affection for Gandhi. That flippant remark was made by Mrs Sarojini Naidu, poet, politician and one of Bapu's intimates (she sometimes called him Mickey Mouse); but she could hardly have been aware at the time of the almost prophetic significance of her words. They actually referred to her loyal efforts to collect money for Gandhi's campaign for *khadi*, homespun cloth. Like all his crusades, it was intended to serve both practical and symbolic purposes. Its practical aspect was the boycott of foreign goods, primarily of English textiles, combined with the fantastic hope of solving India's economic problems by bringing back the handloom and the spinning-wheel. At the same time, on another plane, the spinning-wheel became an almost mystical symbol of the return to the Simple Life, and the rejection of industrialization.

The call of the spinning-wheel, Gandhi wrote in *Young India*, is

* First published in the *Sunday Times*, 5 October 1969, commemorating the centenary of Gandhi's birth.

221

the noblest of all. Because it is the call of love . . . The spinning-wheel is the reviving draught for the millions of our dying countrymen and countrywomen . . . I claim that in losing the spinning-wheel we lost our left lung. We are therefore suffering from galloping consumption. The restoration of the wheel arrests the progress of the fell disease . . .[2]

The wheel was a lifelong obsession which reached its climax in the late 1920s between two imprisonments. It spread among his followers and ran through the successive stages of a fashion, a cult, a mystique. He designed India's national flag with a spinning-wheel in its centre. He persuaded Congress to resolve that all its members should take up spinning and pay their membership dues in self-spun yarn; office-holders had to deliver 2000 yards of yarn per month. When Congress met in session, its seasoned politicians would listen to the debates while operating their portable spinning-wheels – *tricoteuses* of the non-violent revolution. Schools introduced spinning courses; the plain white cloth and white cap became the uniform of the Indian patriot; Nehru called it 'the livery of freedom', while Gandhi praised the wheel as 'the sacrament of millions' and 'a gateway to my spiritual salvation'. At the same time he organized public bonfires of imported cloth, threw his wife's favourite sari into the flames, and got himself arrested.

One of the few Indian intellectuals who dared to protest against the *khadi* mystique was the poet laureate, Rabindranath Tagore. He was a lifelong admirer of Gandhi, fully aware of his greatness, but also of his crankiness. I shall quote him at some length, because he seems to have realized in a single intuitive flash the basic flaw in Gandhian leadership. In 1921, after a prolonged absence, Tagore had returned to India full of expectations 'to breathe the buoyant breeze of national awakening' – and was horrified by what he saw:

What I found in Calcutta when I arrived depressed me. An oppressive atmosphere seemed to burden the land . . . There was a newspaper which one day had the temerity to disapprove, in a feeble way, of the burning of foreign cloth. The very next day the editor was shaken out of his balance by the agitation of his readers. How long would it take for the fire which was burning cloth to reduce his paper to ashes? . . .

Consider the burning of cloth . . . What is the nature of the call to do this? Is it not another instance of a magical formula? The question of using or refusing cloth of a particular manufacture belongs mainly to economic science. The discussion of the matter by our countrymen should have been in the language of economics. If the country has really come to such a habit of mind that precise thinking has become impossible for it, then our very first fight should be against such a fatal habit, the original sin from which all our ills are flowing. But far from this, we take the course of confirming ourselves in it by relying on the magic formula that foreign cloth is 'impure'. Thus economics is bundled out and a fictitious moral dictum dragged into its place . . . If there be anything worse in wearing a particular kind of cloth, that would be an offence against economics, or hygiene, or aesthetics, but certainly not against morality . . .

The command to burn our foreign clothes has been laid on us. I, for one, am unable to obey it . . . Where Mahatma Gandhi has declared war against the tyranny of the machine which is oppressing the whole world, we are all enrolled under his banner. But we must refuse to accept as our ally the illusion-haunted magic-ridden slave-mentality that is at the root of all the poverty and insult under which our country groans.[3]

Tagore had smelt a holy rat in the *khadi* mystique. The boycott of English textiles could be justified as a measure of economic warfare in a nation's struggle for independence. But this did not apply to other countries, and to call all foreign cloth 'impure' was indeed an appeal to magic-ridden minds. If it were advantageous for India's economy to forsake foreign imports and produce all the textiles it needs, that would still leave the question open whether a return to manufacturing methods predating the industrial revolution was feasible – even if it should be deemed desirable in the name of an idealized Simple Life. But this problem, too, was bypassed by calling the wheel a 'sacrament' and a 'gateway to salvation'. In his reply to Tagore, Gandhi went even further in what one might be tempted to call sanctimonious demagogy – if one were not aware of the pure intentions behind the muddled thinking. Rejecting Tagore's accusation that the *khadi* cult was begotten by mysticism, not by reasoned argument, Gandhi wrote:

> I have again and again appealed to reason, and let me assure him that if happily the country has come to believe in the spinning-wheel as the giver of plenty, it has done so after laborious thinking . . . I do indeed ask the poet to spin the wheel as a sacrament . . . Hunger is the argument that is driving India to the spinning-wheel . . . It was our love of foreign cloth that ousted the wheel from its position of dignity. Therefore I consider it a sin to wear foreign cloth . . . On the knowledge of my sin bursting upon me, I must consign the foreign garments to the flames and thus purify myself, and thenceforth rest content with the rough *khadi* made by my neighbours. On knowing that my neighbours may not, having given up the occupation, take kindly to the spinning-wheel, I must take it up myself and thus make it popular.[4]

Khadi did indeed become a fashionable cult among his ashramites and among active members of Congress – but never among the anonymous millions for whom it was intended. The attempt to make the half-starved masses of the rural population self-supporting by means of the spinning-wheel as a 'giver of plenty' proved to be a dismal and pre-dictable failure. The spinning-wheel found its place on the national flag, but not in the peasants' cottages.

A few years ago, a Member of Parliament in New Delhi said to me wistfully: 'Yes, I do wear *khadi*, as you see – a lot of us in the Congress Party feel that we have to. It costs three times as much as ordinary cotton.'

It took a great deal of money, and an infinitely greater amount of idealism and energy, 'to keep Bapu in poverty'. It is impossible to dismiss the *khadi* crusade as a harmless folly. On the contrary, the wheel as an economic panacea and the gateway to salvation was a central symbol of Gandhi's philosophy and social programme.

His first book, *Hind Swaraj or Indian Home Rule*, was written in 1909, when he was forty. He had already achieved international fame as leader of the Indian community in South Africa and initiator of several non-violent mass movements against racial discrimination. The book was reprinted in 1921 with a new introduction by Gandhi in which he said : 'I withdraw nothing of it.' In 1938, he requested that a new edition should be printed at a nominal price available to all, and wrote yet another introduction, in which he affirmed : 'After the stormy thirty years through which I have since passed, I have seen nothing to make me alter the advice expounded in it.' *Hind Swaraj* may thus be regarded as an authoritative expression of opinions to which he clung to the end, and as a condensed version of Gandhian philosophy. It extols the virtues of Indian civilization, and at the same time passionately denounces the culture of the West.

I believe that the civilization India has evolved is not to be beaten in the world. Nothing can equal the seeds sown by our ancestors. Rome went, Greece shared the same fate, the might of the Pharaohs was broken; Japan has become westernized; of China nothing can be said; but India is still, somehow or other, sound at the foundation. The people of Europe learn their lessons from the writings of the men of Greece or Rome, which exist no longer in their former glory. In trying to learn from them, the Europeans imagine that they will avoid the mistakes of Greece and Rome. Such is their pitiable condition. In the midst of all this India remains immovable and that is her glory . . . Many thrust their advice upon India, and she remains steady. This is her beauty . . .

India, as so many writers have shown, has nothing to learn from anybody else, and this is as it should be . . . Indian civilization is the best and the European is a nine-days wonder . . . I bear no enmity towards the English, but I do towards their civilization.[5]

His rejection of Western culture in all its aspects was deeply felt, violently emotional, and supported by arguments verging on the absurd. The principal evils of the West were railways, hospitals and lawyers:

Man is so made by nature as to require him to restrict his movements as far as his hands and feet will take him. If we did not rush about from place to place by means of railways and such other maddening conveniences, much of the confusion that arises would be obviated ... God set a limit to a man's locomotive ambition in the construction of his body. Man immediately proceeded to discover means of overriding the limit ... I am so constructed that I can only serve my immediate neighbours, but in my conceit, I pretend to have discovered that I must with my body serve every individual in the Universe. In thus attempting the impossible, man comes in contact with different religions and is utterly confounded. According to this reasoning, it must be apparent to you that railways are a most dangerous institution. Man has gone further away from his Maker.[6]

If this line of argument were accepted, not only the Great Indian Peninsular Railway would stand condemned, but also Gandhi's favourite book, the *Bhagavad Gita*. For its hero is the noble Arjuna, who drives a chariot (with Vishnu as his passenger) in flagrant transgression of God's will that he should only move as far as his own feet will take him. Gandhi himself had to spend an inordinate proportion of his life in railway carriages 'rushing from place to place', faithful to the tradition that the leader should remain in touch with the masses. It was not the only paradox in his life; in fact, every major principle in Gandhi's Back-to-Nature philosophy was self-defeating, stamped with a tragic irony. (Even as President of Congress, he always insisted on travelling third-class; but he had a special coach to himself.)

Lawyers fare no better in Gandhi's programme than railways:

Men were less unmanly if they settled their disputes either by fighting or by asking their relatives to decide them. They became more unmanly and cowardly when they resorted to the Courts of Law. It is a sign of savagery to settle disputes by fighting. It is not the less so by asking a third party to decide between you and me. The parties alone know who is right and therefore they ought to settle it.[7]

It should be remembered that Gandhi's first step towards leadership was achieved by his successful settling of a lawsuit as an attorney in Pretoria; and his successes in negotiating with the British were as much due to the charisma of the 'naked fakir' – to quote Churchill – as to the legal astuteness of the 'Middle Temple lawyer'.

Perhaps the main asset in the complex balance-sheet of the British Raj was the introduction of modern medicine to India. But in Gandhi's accounting, hospitals fare worst:

> How do diseases arise? Surely by our negligence or indulgence. I over-eat, I have indigestion, I go to a doctor, he gives me medicine. I am cured. I over-eat again, and I take his pills again. Had I not taken the pills in the first instance, I would have suffered the punishment deserved by me, and I would not have over-eaten again . . .
>
> I have indulged in vice, I contract a disease, a doctor cures me, the odds are that I shall repeat the vice. Had the doctor not intervened, nature would have done its work, and I would have acquired mastery over myself, would have been freed from vice, and would have become happy.
>
> Hospitals are institutions for propagating sin. Men take less care of their bodies, and immorality increases.[8]

And in a letter to a friend, also written when he was forty:

> Hospitals are the instruments that the devil has been using for his own purpose, in order to keep his hold on his kingdom. They perpetuate vice, misery and degradation and real slavery.[9]

He tried to live up to his convictions by experimenting all his life with nature-cures, ayurvedic remedies, and an endless succession of vegetarian and fruitarian diets. But he was assailed at various times by fistulae, appendicitis, malaria, hook-worm, amoebic dysentery and high blood-pressure, and suffered two nervous breakdowns in his late sixties. Each time he was seriously ill he started on nature-cures, refusing Western medication and surgery; each time he had to capitulate and submit to drugs, injections, operations under anaesthesia. Once more his principles proved to be self-defeating in the most painful way. Yet while his belief that diseases are caused by 'negligence, indulgence or vice' was naïve to a degree, its correlate, the belief in the power of mind over body, was a source of strength which carried him through his heroic fasts.

About schools and 'literary education' in general he was as scornful as about hospitals, railways and law courts.

> What is the meaning of education? It simply means knowledge of letters. It is merely an instrument and an instrument may be well used or abused . . . We daily observe that many men abuse it and very few make good use of it; and if this is a correct statement, we have proved that more harm has been done by it than good . . .
>
> To teach boys reading, writing and arithmetic is called primary education. A peasant earns his bread honestly. He has ordinary knowledge of the world. He knows fairly well how he should behave towards his parents, his wife, his children and his fellow villagers. He understands and observes the rules of morality. But he cannot write his own name. What do you propose to do by giving him a knowledge of letters? Will you add an inch to his happiness? Do you wish to make him discontented with his cottage or his lot?
>
> Now let us take higher education. I have learned Geography, Astronomy, Algebra, Geometry, etc. What of that? In what way have I benefited myself or those around me? . . .
>
> I do not for one moment believe that my life would have been wasted, had I not received higher or lower education . . . And, if I am making good use of it, even then it is not for the millions . . .
>
> Our ancient school system is enough . . . To give millions a knowledge of English is to enslave them. The foundation that Macaulay laid of education has enslaved us . . . Hypocrisy, tyranny, etc., have increased; English-knowing Indians have not hesitated to cheat or strike terror into the people . . .[10]

Gandhi tried to live up to his principles, and never sent his sons to school. He intended to teach them himself, but did not find the time. They never had a chance to learn a profession. In his own words:

> I will not say that I was indifferent to their literary education, but I certainly did not hesitate to sacrifice it in these higher

interests, as I regarded them. My sons have therefore some reason for grievance against me . . . Had I been able to devote at least one hour to their literary education, with strict regularity, I should have given them, in my opinion, an ideal education. But it has been my regret that I failed to ensure for them enough training in that direction . . . But I hold that I sacrificed their literary training to what I genuinely believed to be a service to the Indian community . . . All my sons have had complaints to make against me in this matter. Whenever they come across an M.A. or a B.A., or even a matriculate, they seem to feel the handicap of a want of school education. Nevertheless I am of opinion that, if I had insisted on their being educated somehow at schools, they would have been deprived of the training that can be had only at the school of experience, or from constant contact with the parents . . .[11]

I shall return presently to the effects this contact had on Gandhi's sons. In the public domain, his hostility to intellectuals with an English education who 'enslaved India' did not prevent him from adopting as his political successor young Jawaharlal Nehru, a product of Harrow and Cambridge. If Western civilization was poison for India, Gandhi had installed the chief poisoner as his heir.

From his early thirties, two ideas of overwhelming, obsessive power were uppermost in Gandhi's mind and dominated his life: *satyagraha* and *brahmacharya*. *Satyagraha* means, broadly, non-violent action; *brahmacharya*, sexual abstinence; but both terms, as we shall see, had for him much wider spiritual implications. The two were inextricably interwoven in his teaching, and more bizarrely in his private life. Significantly it was in the same year – 1906, when he was thirty-seven – that he took his vow of chastity for life, and started his first non-violent campaign.

Gandhi's negative attitude to sex was reminiscent of, and partly inspired by, Tolstoy's, but was more violent and baffling. A partial explanation of its origins may perhaps be the famous episode, related in his autobiography, of his father dying while he had intercourse with his wife. He was sixteen then (having married at fourteen), and had spent the evening, as usual, ministering to his sick father – massaging his feet – when his uncle relieved him. What could be more natural than that he should join his young wife? A few minutes later, however, a servant knocked at the door, announcing the father's death – which apparently nothing had presaged:

I ran to my father's room. I saw that, if animal passion had not blinded me, I should have been spared the torture of separation from my father during his last moments. I should have been massaging him, and he would have died in my arms . . .

This shame of my carnal desire even at the critical hour of my father's death . . . was a blot I have never been able to efface or forget . . . It took me long to get free from the shackles of lust, and I had to pass through many ordeals before I could overcome it.[12]

How much this episode contributed to Gandhi's attitude to sex is a matter of speculation. But the effects of that attitude on his own sons are on record. He refused to send them to school because he wanted to mould them in his own image; and since he had renounced sex, he expected them to do the same. When Harilal, the eldest son, wanted to marry at the age of eighteen, Gandhi refused permission and disowned him 'for the present'. Harilal had the courage to marry nevertheless – he had achieved a degree of independence from his father by living with relatives in India while Gandhi still lived in South Africa. When his wife died in the influenza epidemic of 1918 Harilal, who was now thirty, wanted to remarry; but again Gandhi objected. From that point onward, Harilal began to disintegrate. He became an alcoholic, associated with prostitutes, embraced the Moslem faith and published an attack on his father under the pen-name 'Abdullah'. When he became involved in a shady business transaction, a solicitor wrote a letter of complaint to Gandhi. Gandhi published the lawyer's letter in his paper, *Young India* (18 June 1925), together with his own reply, which amounted to placing Harilal on a public pillory:

I do indeed happen to be the father of Harilal M. Gandhi. He is my eldest boy, is over thirty-six years old and is father of four children. His ideas and mine having been discovered over fifteen years ago to be different, he has been living separately from me . . . Harilal was naturally influenced by the Western veneer that my life at one time did have. His commercial undertakings were totally independent of me . . . He was and still is ambitious. He wants to become rich, and that too easily . . . I do not know how his affairs stand at the moment, except that they are in a bad way . . . Men may be good, not necessarily their children[13]

Father and son hardly ever met again. On her deathbed, Gandhi's wife, Kasturbai, asked for her first-born. Harilal came, drunk, and had to be removed from her presence; 'she wept and beat her forehead'.

He was also present at Gandhi's cremation. Although it is the duty and privilege of the eldest son to light his father's funeral pyre, he kept, or was kept, in the background. He died a month later in a hospital for tuberculosis. His name is rarely mentioned in the voluminous Gandhi literature.

Harilal may have been a difficult case under any circumstances, but the second son, Manilal, was not; he remained a loyal and devoted son to the end. Nevertheless, the way Gandhi treated him was just as inhuman – there is no other word for it. At the age of twenty, Manilal committed the unforgivable sin of losing his virginity to a woman. When Gandhi discovered this he made a public scene, went on a penitential fast, and decreed that he would never allow Manilal to marry. He even managed to persuade the guilty woman to shave her hair. A full fifteen years had to pass until Gandhi relented, on Kasturbai's entreaties, and gave his permission for Manilal to marry – by which time Manilal was thirty-five. But in the meantime he had been banished from Gandhi's presence and ashram, because he had lent some money, out of his own savings, to his disgraced brother Harilal. When Gandhi heard about it, he made a scene accusing Manilal of dishonesty, on the grounds that the ashrimites' savings were the property of the ashram. Manilal was sent into exile with instructions to become a weaver's apprentice, and not to use the name Gandhi. 'In addition to this,' Manilal later told Louis Fischer, 'Father also contemplated a fast, but I sat all night entreating him not to do so, and in the end my prayer was heeded. I left my dear mother and my brother Devadas sobbing . . .'[14] After a year as a weaving-apprentice and a publisher's assistant, Gandhi ordered him to Natal to edit *Indian Opinion*. Apart from visits, Manilal remained an exile to the end of Gandhi's life.

In fairness, Gandhi's treatment of his two eldest sons must be seen in the context of the traditional Hindu joint family household, over which the father holds unrestricted sway. To go against his decisions is unthinkable; as long as Bapu is alive, the sons are not regarded as having attained fully adult status. But even against this background Gandhi's relentless tyranny over his sons was exceptional – he rode them like the djinn of the Arab legend, whom, in the guise of an old man, his young victim cannot get off his shoulders. 'I was a slave of passion when Harilal was conceived,' he was wont to say. 'I had a carnal and luxurious life during Harilal's childhood.' Quite clearly he was visiting his own sins on his sons. By his efforts to prevent them from marrying, he was trying to deprive them of their manhood, convinced that he had a right to do so, since he had voluntarily renounced his own. Their crime, which he could never forgive, was that they refused to follow him on the lofty path of *brahmacharya*.

This becomes even more evident by comparing the way he treated them with the favours bestowed on a young second cousin, Maganlal. 'Maganlal is dearer to me than one who is a son because so born,' Gandhi wrote to his brother. And while his own sons were not allowed to go to school, he sent Maganlal (and another young second cousin) to study in England. Why this contrast? When Maganlal died at the age of forty-five, Gandhi explained the reason in his obituary: 'He whom I had singled out as heir to my all is no more. He closely studied and followed my spiritual career, and when I presented to my co-workers *brahmacharya* as a rule of life, even for married men in search of Truth, he was the first to perceive the beauty and necessity of the practice.'[15]

Gandhi almost invariably refers to the act of love as an expression of man's 'carnal lust' or 'animal passion', and to woman's role in the act as that of a 'victim' or 'object'. He did know, of course, that women too have a sexual urge, but had a simple answer to that: 'Let her transfer her love . . . to the whole of humanity, let her forget she ever was or ever can be the object of man's lust.'[16] Intercourse, he taught, was only permissible for the purpose of procreation; if indulged in for 'carnal satisfaction', it is a 'reversion to animality'. Accordingly, he unconditionally rejected birth-control, even within the limits permitted by the Catholic Church. When Dr Margaret Sanger, the pioneer of family-planning, visited Gandhi in 1936, she talked about the catastrophic consequences of the population explosion in India and elsewhere, and appealed for his help, pleading that 'there are thousands, millions, who regard your word as that of a saint'. But throughout their conversation 'he held to an idea or a train of thought of his own, and, as soon as you stopped, continued it as though he had not heard you . . . Despite his claim to open-mindedness, he was proud of not altering his opinions . . . He accused himself of being a brute by having desired his wife when he was younger, and classed all sex relations as debasing acts, although sometimes necessary for procreation. He agreed that no more than three or four children should be born to a family, but insisted that intercourse, therefore, should be restricted for the entire married life of the couple to three or four occasions.'[17]

As a solution to India's population problem this was about as realistic as the return of the spinning-wheel. Yet it was deeply rooted in Gandhi's religious beliefs. If *khadi* was the gateway to salvation, *brahmacharya* was 'the conduct that leads to God' – which is what the word literally means. Thus, to quote his secretary and biographer Pyarelal, '*Brahmacharya* came to occupy the place of honour in Gandhiji's discipline for *satyagraha* . . . It was the *sine qua non* for those who aspire to a spiritual of higher life'[18] – and thus for all ashrimites, married or not. How deeply he felt about this is illustrated by an episode in Gandhi's first ashram – Phoenix Settlement in South Africa:

> Once when I was in Johannesburg I received the tidings of the moral fall of two of the inmates of the ashram. News of an apparent failure or reverse in the [political] struggle would not shock me, but this news came upon me like a thunderbolt. The same day I took the train for Phoenix. Mr Kallenbach insisted on accompanying me. He had noticed the state I was in. He would not brook the thought of my going alone, for he happened to be the bearer of the tidings which had so upset me. On the way my duty became clear to me. I felt that the guardian or the teacher was responsible, to some extent, at least, for the lapse of his pupil . . . I also felt that the parties to the guilt could be made to realize my distress and the depth of their fall only if I did some penance for it. So I imposed upon myself a fast for seven days and a vow of having only one meal for a period of four months and a half. Mr Kallenbach tried to dissuade me, but in vain. He ultimately accepted the propriety of the penance and insisted on joining me . . . Thus considerably relieved, I reached Phoenix. I made further investigation and acquainted myself with some more details I needed to know. My penance pained everybody, but it cleared the atmosphere. Everyone came to realize what a terrible thing it was to be sinful.[19]

This episode – including the reaction of the unfortunate Mr Kallenbach – gives one a foretaste of the curious atmosphere that prevailed in Gandhi's later ashrams. Whereas in politics Gandhi always tended towards compromise, in the matter of *brahmacharya* he became more fanatical as the years went by. He used his proverbial fascination for women to persuade them to take the vow, whether their husbands agreed or not, wrecking several marriages in the process, and causing lasting unhappiness in others (among them is the sad case of a personal friend). One might say that the young women who came under his spell were seduced by Gandhi into chastity.

The consequences were described by one of Gandhi's intimate collaborators, Professor Nirmal Kumar Bose – one of the few who dared to talk to him in plain words on this subject.

'When women love men in normal life,' he said to the Mahatma, 'a part of their psychological hunger is satisfied by the pleasure which they derive in the physical field. But when women pay their homage of love to you, there can be no such satisfaction, with the result that when they come close to you personally, their mind becomes slightly warped. Of course, all of us are neurotics to a more or less extent. But the effect of your contact has an undoubtedly dangerous influence upon some of your associates, whether male or female.'[20]

Sexual abstinence may procure spiritual benefits to communities of monks or nuns segregated from the opposite sex and carefully sheltered from temptation. But Gandhi had designed for himself a very special and arduous road to *brahmacharya*; he felt compelled to expose himself to temptation in order to test his progress in self-control. He regarded these tests – which continued to the very end when he was nearly eighty – as a pioneering venture, another 'Experiment with Truth' (as he called his autobiography). The experiments started with his own wife after he had taken the vow, and were then continued with other, younger women. In a letter to Bose, justifying these practices, Gandhi wrote:

I am amazed at your assumption that my experiment implied any assumption of woman's inferiority. She would be, if I looked upon her with lust with or without her consent. I have believed in woman's perfect equality with man. My wife was 'inferior' when she was the instrument of my lust. She ceased to be that when she lay with me naked as my sister. If she and I were not lustfully agitated in our minds and bodies, the contact raised both of us.

Should there be a difference if it is not my wife, as she once was, but some other sister? I do hope you will acquit me of having any

235

lustful designs upon women or girls who have been naked with me. A or B's hysteria had nothing to do with my experiment, I hope. They were before the experiment what they are today, if they have not less of it.

The distinction between Manu and others is meaningless for our discussion . . . [21]

The Manu mentioned in this letter was the granddaughter of a cousin, the last of the guinea-pigs in the quest for *brahmacharya*. She had lost her mother in childhood, and Kasturbai had looked after her. On Kasturbai's death Gandhi took over. 'I have been a father to many, but only to you I am a mother,'[22] he wrote to her; strange as this may sound, he meant her to take that literally – so much so that Manu actually wrote a book with the title *Bapu: My Mother*. As a 'budding girl of eighteen', in Gandhi's words, she claimed to be free from sexual feelings. However, as Pyarelal explains in his biography:

Gandhiji had come to have an uneasy feeling that either she did not know her own mind or she was deceiving herself and others. As a 'mother' he must know . . . girls often conceal their real feelings from their fathers but not from their mothers. Gandhiji had claimed that he was mother to her and she had endorsed the claim. If the truth of it could be tested, it would provide a clue to the problem that baffled him. Incidentally, it would enable him also to know how far he had advanced on the road to perfect *brahmacharya* – complete sexlessness . . . He did for her everything that a mother usually does for her daughter. He supervised her education, her food, dress, rest and sleep. For closer supervision and guidance he made her share the same bed with him. Now a girl, if her mind is perfectly innocent, never feels embarrassment in sleeping with her mother.[23]

To paraphrase Sarojini Naidu: it took a great deal of derring-do to keep Bapu in chastity.

Manu apparently did not feel any embarrassment. She returned his ministrations by nursing him through illnesses and fasts; in her diary she recorded, in between two political messages, the effects of the enema she had administered to him, and the admonitions he addressed to her from his bath-tub: 'While bathing, Bapu said these words to me with great affection, and also caressed my back'.[24] But in view of the traditional lack of privacy in India, and in particular among ashramites, such intimacies could be exchanged in relative innocence.

For Gandhi it was a crucial experiment. If it succeeded 'it would show that his quest for truth had been successful. *His sincerity should then impress itself upon the Moslems, his opponents in the Moslem League and even Jinnah,* who doubted his sincerity, to their own and India's harm.'[25] The italics are by the faithful Pyarelal who knew more intimately than any other contemporary the ways and twists of his Master's thought. Gandhi sincerely believed that he was an instrument of God, who 'gives me guidance to react to the situations as they arise'.[26] But the instrument must be pure, free from carnal desire; and to attain that freedom he had to go through his experiment in *brahmacharya.* It 'put him in touch with the infinite'[27]; at the same time it was to solve the Hindu–Moslem problem, put an end to the mutual massacres, persuade the Moslem League of his *bona fides,* and make them renounce their claim for an independent Pakistan.

From the Mahatma's point of view all this was perfectly logical. In his own mind, his public, political activities and his intimate Experiments with Truth were inseparable; *satyagraha* and *brahmacharya* were mutually interdependent. For *satyagraha* means not only non-violent action, but action powered by an irresistible soul-force or truth-force (*sat—* truth, *agraha* – firmness). At the stage he had reached in the last two years of his life everything depended for him on the crucial experiment with Manu; and this may explain why he so stubbornly insisted that she share his bed, in defiance of everybody's advice.

It also explains why, while the fate of India was being decided in the dramatic months June–July 1947, Gandhi chose to treat the Indian public to a series of six articles – on *brahmacharya.* He had been touring the Moslem villages of east Bengal, attempting to quell the riots by his personal influence. Most of the time, his only companions on the pilgrimage were Manu, Bose and a stenographer. Several of his collaborators, including intimate friends, protested against the Manu experiment (though they must have known of previous ones), expressed their disapproval to Gandhi, and some of them actually left him. A public scandal was avoided, but Gandhi felt deprived of their unconditional admiration, utterly lonely and dejected. Even Bose left, after long discussions in which he had in vain tried to convince Gandhi of the psychological ill-effects of the experiment on both parties concerned – without ever doubting the sincerity of their motives; but he returned to serve Gandhi a few months later. The ill-timed *Harijan* articles, which made the public gasp, were Gandhi's reply to the dissidents.

He also wrote to Acharya Kripalani, the President of Congress: 'This is a very personal letter, but not private. Manu Gandhi, my granddaughter . . . shares the bed with me . . . This has cost me dearest associates . . . I have given the deepest thought to the matter. The whole world may forsake me, but I dare not leave what I hold is the truth for me . . . I have risked perdition before now. Let this be the reality if it has to be.'[28] And he requests that the Acharya discuss the matter with other Congress politicians – in the midst of the negotiations about independence.

I have dwelt at some length on Gandhi's struggles to attain chastity for two reasons; because it provides an essential – by his own testimony, the most essential – key to his personality; and because it became a part of the Gandhian heritage which had a lasting influence on the social and cultural climate of the country.

After Gandhi's death, however, the Indian Establishment attempted to suppress the facts of his last Experiment with Truth. An example of this conspiracy of silence is the story of the book by Nirmal Kumar Bose, *My Days with Gandhi*, which I have repeatedly quoted. Professor Bose, a distinguished anthropologist and expounder of Gandhi's philosophy, had written two earlier books, *Studies in Gandhism* and *Selections from Gandhi*. He had been the Mahatma's companion during the pilgrimage in East Bengal, and in *My Days with Gandhi* devoted a chapter to the repercussions of the Manu experiments, without going into details about the experiment itself. It is a discreet, affectionate and respectful work; yet not only was it rejected by all publishers whom Bose approached, but strenuous attempts were made 'from very high quarters in the country' to prevent its publication.

Five years after Gandhi's death, Bose decided to publish the book on his own. It is unobtainable in India, and the most recent biographer of Gandhi, Geoffrey Ashe, remarks: 'It has become common knowledge that one important memoir was partly suppressed. I had some difficulty in locating what may be the only copy in England'.[29] Not even the British Museum has a copy of it. A book of my own,[30] in which I quoted Bose, was also banned in India on the grounds that it contained 'disrespectful remarks about Gandhiji'. (As a reaction to the ban, an Indian reader sent me a complete xerox copy of Bose's book.)

Ironically, three years after Bose, the first volume of Pyarelal's monumental, authorized biography of Gandhi was published, confirming all the facts that Bose had mentioned (but without mentioning Bose). The following passage from *My Days with Gandhi* is relevant in this context:

There are many who were close to Gandhiji and who knew about these happenings, but who, out of a fear of misrepresenting him, have thought it wiser to leave out this portion of his life from any critical consideration at all. But the present writer has always felt that such an attitude is not justified. Perhaps away at the back of our minds there is a lurking belief that what Gandhiji did was not right; and, in an apparent effort of avoiding injustice to his greatness, we may perhaps decide to draw a veil over certain events of which we have personal knowledge. But this can only be achieved by sacrificing what I believe to be one of the most important keys to an understanding of this unique personality of our age.

... We can only bear testimony to what we have witnessed; and, in a spirit of utter truthfulness, describe it with the utmost fidelity possible ... So that when our age has passed away and many of the values for which we stand have been relegated to the lumber-heap of history, men may have the means of knowing all that is possible about a man who once stood towering like a mountain above those who lived beside him.[31]

In the Western world Gandhi's obsession with *brahmacharya* could have been shrugged off as a harmless personal quirk. In India it struck deep, archetypal chords. There is a hidden message running through Gandhi's preaching of chastity – hidden that is from the Western reader, but obvious to every Hindu. It relates to the physiological benefits of sexual restraint. According to the doctrines of traditional Hindu (*ayurvedic*) medicine, man's 'vital force' is concentrated in his seminal fluid. All his powers, both mental and physical, derive from this precious secretion – a kind of elixir of life – variously called *bindu*, *soma-rasa* or 'vital fluid'. Every expenditure of 'vital fluid' causes physical weakening and spiritual impoverishment. Conversely, the storing up of *bindu* through continence provides for increased spiritual powers, health and longevity (Gandhi hoped to live to the age of 125). It also produces that smooth skin with a radiant glow which all true saints were said to possess – including the Mahatma. Various semi-secret Hatha Yoga practices are designed to preserve the vital fluid even during intercourse.

Gandhi was a firm believer in *ayurvedic* medicine, and himself practised it on his family and intimates. Numerous passages in his writings show that he also believed in the crucial importance of preserving the 'vital fluid'. Thus in his pamphlet 'Key to Health' he wrote:

It is said that an impotent man is not free from sexual desire ... But the cultivated impotence of the man whose sexual desire has been burnt up and whose sexual secretions are being converted into vital force is wholly different. It is to be desired by everybody.[32]

Or:

Ability to retain and assimilate the vital liquid is a matter of long training. Once achieved, it strengthens body and mind. The vital liquid capable of producing such a wonderful being as man cannot but, when properly conserved, be transmuted into matchless energy and strength.[33]

Hinduism has a notoriously ambivalent attitude towards sex. On the one hand, the cult of the *lingam*, the erotic temple carvings, the *Kama Sutra* and the 'Sex Pharmacies' with their flowering trade in aphrodisiacs; on the other, prudery, hypocrisy, lip-service to the ideal of chastity combined with anxiety about the loss of the vital fluid and its debilitating effects. 'Spermal anxiety' appears to be common among Hindus; and with it goes unconscious resentment against Woman who is its cause. The Hindu Pantheon has no Eros and no Cupids – only Kama, the prime force of lust.

Typical of this attitude is a correspondent's letter to Gandhi complaining that he was unable to live up to the ideal of chastity, 'although I often say to myself why enter the muck-hole at all?' Equally typical is Gandhi's reply: 'I can only detect ignorance in likening women to a muck-pot. The very thought is insulting to both men and woman. May not her son sit side by side with his mother, or the man share the same bench in a train with his sister?' His defence of woman is confined to her role as mother and sister, but not as a wife; by implication Gandhi shared his correspondent's view. 'If women only knew how to resist their husbands all would be well,' he remarked bitterly to Margaret Sanger. 'I have been able to teach women who have come in contact with me how to resist their husbands. The real problem is that many do not want to resist them . . .'[34]

Gandhi's lifelong struggle to overcome his own 'carnal lust' and 'animal passion'; his public *mea culpa* when he confessed to a 'lust dream' followed by a penance of six weeks' silence; his endorsement of the power of the 'vital fluid' – all this made him the living symbol of the guilt-ridden Hindu

R

attitude to sex, and encouraged the worshipful masses to persist in it. As a result, the trade in aphrodisiacs is thriving as before, surrounded by the odour of sanctimonious hypocrisy.

A minor but significant feature of the Gandhian heritage is the widespread hypochondria about diet and digestion. In a country riddled with amoebic dysentery, hook-worm and other scourges, this is not surprising. But Gandhi's lifelong preoccupation with experimental diets was again primarily linked with the quest for chastity. When he took the vow, he wrote: 'Control of the palate is the first essential in the observance of the vow . . . The *brahmacharya*'s food should be limited, simple, spiceless and if possible uncooked . . . Six years of experiment have shown me that the *brahmacharya*'s ideal food is fresh fruit and nuts.'[35] Even milk he thought was an aphrodisiac to be avoided – which seems difficult to reconcile with the pamphlet he wrote on 'How to Serve the Cow'.[36]

One of Gandhi's biographers, Louis Fischer, called him 'a unique person, a great person, perhaps the greatest figure of the last nineteen hundred years'. Others compared him to Christ, Buddha and St Francis. The claims to immortality were based on his use of non-violence as a political weapon in a world sick of violence. The partial success of his early passive resistance, civil disobedience and non-co-operation campaigns; the unarmed marches against armed police and troops; the first sit-downs, the cheerful courting of imprisonment, the public fasts – all this was something completely new in politics, something unheard of; it was a message of hope, almost a revelation; and the amazing thing was that it seemed to work. The lasting merit of Gandhi was, not that he 'liberated India' – as John Grigg[37] and others have pointed out, independence would have come much earlier without him – but to have made the world realize that the conventional methods of power-politics are not the only conceivable ones; and that under certain circumstances non-violence – *ahimsa* – might be substituted for them. But the emphasis is on the limiting clause; and the tragedy of Gandhi was the narrow range of applicability of his method. It was a noble game which could only be played against an adversary abiding by certain rules of common decency instilled by long tradition; otherwise it would amount to mass suicide.

Like most inventors of a new philosophical system, Gandhi at first believed in its universal validity. The earliest shock of disappointment came in 1919, when the first nation-wide civil disobedience campaign degenerated into violent rioting all over the country. Gandhi suspended the action, went on a penitential fast, and confessed to having committed a 'Himalayan blunder' by starting the campaign before his followers had been sufficiently trained in the spirit and methods of *satyagraha*.

The next year he launched a new non-co-operation movement, jointly with the Moslems. Again it led to nation-wide riots, culminating in the massacre of Chauri Chaura; again he suspended the campaign and went on a fast.

His most successful movement was the civil disobedience campaign in 1930–31 against the salt laws, highlighted by the spectacular 'march to the sea'. This time, too, there was widespread rioting, but the campaign was allowed to continue until a compromise settlement was reached with the Viceroy.

The later *satyagraha* movements (1932–4, 1940–41 and 1942–3) ended inconclusively. In terms of tangible results this was not an impressive record. But the general impact on politicians, intellectuals and the world at large was momentous; it turned Gandhi into a living legend. It was further dramatized by his eighteen public fasts and altogether six-and-a-half years of detention – the first in a black hole in Johannesburg, the last in the Aga Khan's palace.

But Gandhi's methods of using non-violence had their Himalayan inconsistencies, and the advice he proffered to

243

other nations was often quite irresponsible by any humane standard. Although he repeated over and again that only people far advanced on the spiritual trail were able to practise non-violent resistance, he did not hesitate to recommend it as a universal panacea, even in such tragically inappropriate situations as that of the German Jews under the Nazis. In December 1938, after the first nation-wide pogrom, he wrote: 'I make bold to say that, if the Jews can summon to their aid soul-power that comes only from non-violence, Herr Hitler will bow before the courage which he will own is infinitely superior to that shown by his best stormtroopers.'[38] And in 1946, when the incredible news of six million gassed victims became known: 'The Jews should have offered themselves to the butcher's knife. They should have thrown themselves into the sea from cliffs . . . It would have roused the world and the people of Germany.'[39]

There was only one mitigating circumstance to utterances like this: Gandhi's notorious ignorance of international affairs.

At the outbreak of the Second World War he declared his moral support for the Allied cause. After the fall of France, he praised Pétain for his courage to surrender, and on 6 July 1940 published an 'Appeal to Every Briton' to follow the French example (on his insistence, the text of this appeal was transmitted by the Viceroy to the British War Cabinet):

. . . I do not want Britain to be defeated nor do I want her to be victorious in a trial of brute strength . . . I want you to fight Nazism without arms or with non-violent arms. I would like you to lay down the arms you have, being useless for your humanity. You will invite Herr Hitler and Signor Mussolini to take what they want of the countries you call your possessions. Let them take possession of your beautiful island, with your many beautiful buildings. You will give all these, but neither your souls, nor your minds. If these gentlemen choose to occupy your homes, you will vacate them. If they do not give you free passage out, you will allow yourself, man, woman and child, to be slaughtered, but you will refuse to owe allegiance to them.[40]

It would have taken a great deal of corpses to keep Bapu in non-violence.

He had similar advice to offer to Czechs, Poles, Finns and Chinese. On the last day of his life, a few hours before he was assassinated, a correspondent of *Life* magazine asked him: 'How would you meet the atom bomb . . . with non-violence?' He replied:

'I will not go into shelter. I will come out in the open and let the pilot see I have not a trace of ill-will against him. The pilot will not see our faces from his great height, I know. But the longing in our hearts – that he will not come to harm – would reach up to him and his eyes would be opened.'[41]

This statement, and many earlier ones on similar lines, give the impression that Gandhi's faith in non-violence was absolute ('I know of no single case in which it has failed,' he wrote in his 'Appeal to Every Briton'). In fact, however, on a number of critical occasions he betrayed his own principles in a quite blatant way. There was the episode, not to be taken too seriously, when, in 1918, he acted as a recruiting sergeant for the British Army. In a speech in the Kheda district he said:

To bring about [Dominion status in the Empire] we should have the ability to defend ourselves, that is, the ability to bear arms and to use them . . . If we want to learn the use of arms with the greatest possible despatch, it is our duty to enlist ourselves in the army.[42]

Three years later, he asserted:

Under Independence I too would not hesitate to advise those who would bear arms to do so and fight for the country.[43]

Later on he explained these lapses by saying that they did not imply any lack of faith in non-violence, but merely that 'I had not yet found my feet . . . I was not sufficiently sure of my ground.'[44] But this excuse can hardly be applied to the climactic events in the last two years of his life – the Hindu–Moslem massacres which led to Partition, and the fighting in

Kashmir which signalled the ultimate shipwreck of non-violence. During his pilgrimage through the terror-stricken villages of East Bengal when he saw 'only darkness all round', he confessed to Bose that 'for the time being' he had 'given up searching for a non-violent remedy applicable to the masses'. A few days later, he wrote: 'Violence is horrible and retarding, but may be used in self-defence.' But another few days later, in a letter: 'Non-violent defence is the supreme self-defence, being infallible.'[45]

He was at the end of his tether.

In one of the devastated villages he received the visit of a Moslem divine who had saved the lives of several Hindu families by persuading them to go through a mock ceremony of conversion to Islam. 'Gandhi told them that it would have been much better if, as a religious preceptor, he had taught the Hindus to lay down their lives for their faith rather than give it up through fear. The divine continued to argue that such false conversion for saving one's life had the sanction of religion, when Gandhiji grew impatient and in an almost angry tone said if ever he met God he would ask him why a man with such views had ever been made a religious preceptor. The divine became silent and after an exchange of courtesies left.'[46]

Gandhi had strenuously opposed Partition; he called it 'the vivisection of India which would mean the vivisection of myself'. At the historical meeting of Congress, on 14–15 June 1947, which was to decide for or against Partition, the President, Acharya Kripalani, Gandhi's lifelong friend, made a memorable speech which signified the future Indian Government's farewell to the ideals of non-violence. Unlike Mark Anthony, he started by praising Gandhi, and then proceeded to bury him. He expressed his appreciation of Gandhi's pilgrimages in Bengal and Bihar, trying to bring about Hindu-Moslem reconciliation as an alternative to Partition, but denied the efficacy of the method: 'Unfortunately for us today, though (Gandhi) can enunciate policies, they have to be in the main carried out by others, and these others are not converted to his way of thinking. It is under these painful circumstances that I have supported the division of India.'[47]

To everybody's surprise, Gandhi in his speech suddenly urged acceptance of Partition on the grounds that 'sometimes certain decisions, however unpalatable they may be, have to be taken'. Three months later, independent India and independent Pakistan were confronting each other in Kashmir. Gandhi commented in one of his after-prayer speeches that he had been 'an opponent of all warfare. But if there was no other way of securing justice from Pakistan, if Pakistan persistently refused to see its proved error and continued to minimize it, the Indian Union would have to go to war against it. War was no joke. No one wanted war. That way lay destruction. But he could never advise anyone to put up with injustice.'[48]

'My affection for Gandhi,' Kingsley Martin wrote after his last visit to India, 'and my knowledge that he was a great man were not impaired by the discovery that he was still a Hindu nationalist and an imperfect disciple of the Mahatma.'[49] I am not at all sure whether he would have supported an Indian version of the movement for unilateral nuclear disarmament. He had been lavish with his advice to Britons, Frenchmen, Czechs, Poles, Jews, to lay down their arms and surrender to injustices infinitely more terrible than those committed by Pakistan. As on earlier critical occasions, when the lofty ideal clashed with hard reality, realism carried the day and the Yogi succumbed to the Commissar. He had believed in and practised nature medicine, but when critically ill had always called in the practitioners of Western science which he held in such contempt. *Ahimsa* and *satyagraha* had worked like magic on the British, but did not work on Moslems. Was it really the panacea for mankind as he had thought? A fortnight before his death, commenting on Deputy Premier Sirdar Patel's decision to send troops into Kashmir, Gandhi confessed to Bose:

When power descended on [Patel], he saw that he could no longer successfully apply the method of non-violence which he used to wield with signal success. I have made the discovery that what I and the people with me termed non-violence was not the genuine article, but a weak copy known as passive resistance. Naturally, passive resistance can avail nothing to a ruler.[50]

To another interviewer – Professor Stuart Nelson – he repeated that 'what he had mistaken for *satyagraha* was not more than passive resistance, which was a weapon of the weak . . . Gandhiji proceeded to say that it was indeed true that he had all along laboured under an illusion. But he was never sorry for it. He realized that if his vision had not been clouded by that illusion, India would never have reached the point which it had done today.'[51]

Yet that, too, may have been no more than an illusion. India had reached the point of independence not because of *ahimsa*, but because the Empire had gone into voluntary self-liquidation. The spinning-wheel was preserved on its national flag, but the Gandhian mystique played no part in the shaping of the new state, though it continued to pay lip-service to it. The armed conflicts with Pakistan and China produced outbreaks of chauvinism and mass hysteria which suggested that the Mahatma's pacifist apostolate had left hardly any tangible effects; and the repeated, bloody riots between Maharatis and Gandhi's own Gujeratis added a bitterly ironic touch to the picture. When Gandhi's adopted spiritual heir, Vinoba Bhave, 'the marching saint', was asked whether he approved of armed resistance against the Chinese frontier intrusion, he replied in the affirmative, using Gandhi's erstwhile excuse that the masses were not yet ripe for non-violent resistance. To paraphrase St Augustine: 'Lord, give us non-violence, but not yet.'

Gandhi himself foresaw this development in moments when his vision was not 'clouded by illusion'. On the day Independence was proclaimed, 15 August 1947, when the whole world awaited his message on this historic occasion, he refused to send one. Emissaries of the newly formed government pointed out to him that his silence would create a bad impression. He replied: 'If it is bad, let it be so . . .' Bose noted in his diary: 'He said, there was a time when India listened to him. Today he was a back number. He was told that he had no place in the new order where they wanted machines, navy, air force, and what-not. He could never be party to that.' Towards the end, attendance at his prayer-meetings dwindled appreciably, and the after-prayer speeches 'failed to evoke the same enthusiasm as formerly. His voice seemed to have lost its magic quality.'[52]

Pyarelal was another witness of the final agony. 'One sentence that was constantly on his lips was, "Don't you see, I am mounted on my funeral pyre" . . . Sometimes he asked himself whether he had not become a dead weight on his colleagues and on the country, an anachronism and a misfit in the new era that was shaping around him, and which he had done more than anyone else to shape . . . I watched day after day the wan, sad look on that pinched face, bespeaking an inner anguish that was frightening to behold.'[53]

The principles by which he hoped to shape India, laid down forty years earlier in *Hind Swaraj*, had turned out to be self-defeating. In the midst of the celebrations, their – and his – defeat was complete. It was sealed by an assassin, who was not one from the enemy camp, but a devout Hindu.

J. F. Horrabin has described a meeting with Gandhi at St James's Palace where the Round Table Conference of 1931 was held:

We chatted for some minutes in a small ante-room. Then, catching sight of a clock, he remembered another appointment, apologized, and hurried away. I watched him disappear down one of the long corridors of the Palace; his robes tucked in, his slippers twinkling as he ran. Dare I say it? – I am sure, at least, that no friend of his will misunderstand me if I do – I was irresistibly reminded of one of those Chaplin films which end with the little figure hurrying away to the horizon, gradually lost to sight in the distance.[54]

That remark, far from being disrespectful, leads straight to the secret of Gandhi's immense power over his country-men, and the love they bore him. Chaplin was the symbol of the little man in a bowler hat in the industrialized society of the West. Gandhi was the symbol of the little man in a loincloth in poverty-stricken India. He himself was fully aware of this. When J. P. Patel once asked him 'what it was in him that created such a tremendous following in our country', he replied, 'It's the man of our country who realizes when he sees me that I am living as he does, and I am a part of his own self.'[55]

Nehru, the westernized progressive, often regarded Gandhi as a political liability, but he was nevertheless under his spell, precisely because Gandhi to him was, in his own words, 'the soul of India'.

The soul and the loincloth went together; they were inseparable. When Gandhi had tea with George V and Queen Mary at Buckingham Palace, wearing sandals, loin-cloth and a shawl on his shoulders, it was more than just showmanship. It was an event which instantly turned into legend, spreading to the remotest villages of India. One version of it was given years later by the Vice-Chancellor of Poonah University, who accompanied Gandhi to the gates of Buckingham Palace: 'He went to see the King dressed in a poor man's costume, with half his legs visible. The King said, "Mr Gandhi, how is India doing?" He said, "Look at me and you will know what India is like."' Every villager with naked legs who felt that Gandhi was 'a part of his own self', thought himself for a moment equal to the King of England. Perhaps Gandhi's greatest gift to his people was to arouse in them, after centuries of lethargy, the first stirrings of self-respect.

But he also gave his blessing to their attitudes, derived from a petrified tradition, to sex, food, paternal authority, medicine, industry and education; and he confirmed them in that 'illusion-haunted, magic-ridden mentality' which Tagore has castigated as 'the original sin from which all our ills are flowing'. Even where he opposed tradition, he did it on the traditional principle of the identity of opposites: the Untouchables became Harijans, Children of God; the sources of defilement were turned into objects of worship, and latrine-cleaning became a sacrament for all pious ashramites – though for nobody else.

Gandhi exerted such a powerful influence over the minds of the masses that many believed him to be an Avatar, a reincarnation of Krishna. One cannot help feeling that had he crusaded for family-planning instead of the impossible demand for married continence, India might be a different country now. He was most eloquent about the poverty-stricken life of the Indian villager and his inability to feed the exorbitant numbers of his offspring; but the only remedy he had to propose was chastity and the spinning-wheel.

He was unwilling to listen to the reasoned arguments of critics. In the words of T. A. Raman, a distinguished Indian journalist: 'Almost the most marked trait of Gandhi's character is that evidenced by the virtual impossibility of reasoning with him. By definition he is a man of faith, and men of faith have little use for the slow processes of reasoning ... This, and the unshakable conviction of his own right-ness, make arguments with Gandhi pleasant (for he is a good listener) but futile.'[56]

It is equally pleasant but futile to argue with intellectuals who adhere to the Gandhi cult and pay lip-service to a philosophy easy to eulogize and impossible to realize. It is this attitude which lends the contemporary Indian scene its twilight air of unreality, muddleheadedness and sancti-monious evasion of vital issues. Bapu still casts his saintly–sickly spell over it, but its power is waning as more people realize that, whether we like it or not, spinning-wheels cannot compete with factories, and that the most vital fluid is the water from large, modern irrigation dams for the country's parched fields.

When all is said, the Mahatma, in his humble and heroic ways, was the greatest living anachronism of the twentieth century; and one cannot help feeling, blasphemous though it may sound, that India would be better off today and healthier in mind, without the Gandhian heritage.

REFERENCES

1. Geoffrey Ashe, *Gandhi : A Study in Revolution* (London, 1968), p. 267.
2. In Homer A. Jack, ed., *The Gandhi Reader : A Source-Book of his Life and Writings* (London, 1958), pp. 229–30.
3. ibid., pp. 223, 225, 226.
4. ibid., pp. 228–31.
5. ibid., pp. 107–8, 120.
6. Sir C. Sankaran Nair, *Gandhi and Anarchy* (Madras, 1922), pp. 4–5.
7. ibid., p. 6.
8. ibid., pp. 6–7.
9. ibid., p. 18.
10. M. K. Gandhi, *Hind Swaraj or Indian Home Rule* (Ahmedabad, 1939, reprinted 1946), pp. 63–6.
11. C. F. Andrews, *Mahatma Gandhi : His Own Story* (London, 1930, 2 vols.), pp. 94–5.
12. M. K. Gandhi, *My Experiments with Truth* (London, 1949), pp. 167–8.
13. ibid., p. 26.
14. Louis Fischer, *The Life of Mahatma Gandhi* (London, 1951), p. 230.
15. ibid., p. 229.
16. Nirmal Kumar Bose, *My Days with Gandhi* (Calcutta, 1953), p. 203.
17. Margaret Sanger, *An Autobiography* (New York, 1938), pp. 470–71.
18. Pyarelal, *Mahatma Gandhi : The Last Phase* (Ahmedabad, 1965, 2 vols.), pp. 570, 579.
19. Andrews, op. cit., p. 186.
20. Bose, op. cit., p. 133.
21. ibid., p. 177.

22. Manuben, Gandhi, *Bapu : My Mother*, trans. from Gujerati by Chitra Desai (Ahmedabad, 1949; 2nd revised edn, 1955), p. 3.
23. Pyarelal, op. cit., p. 575.
24. Manuben, Gandhi, *Last Glimpses of Bapu* (Delhi, Agra and Jaipur, 1962), p. 303.
25. Pyarelal, op. cit., p. 580.
26. T. A. Raman, *What Does Gandhi Want?* (Oxford, New York and Toronto, 1943), p. 49.
27. Bose, op. cit., p. 176.
28. Pyarelal, op. cit., p. 581.
29. Ashe, op. cit., p. viii.
30. *The Lotus and the Robot* (London and New York, 1959).
31. Bose, op. cit., pp. 189–90.
32. Pyarelal, op. cit., p. 571.
33. Fischer, op. cit., p. 263.
34. In Jack, op. cit., pp. 303–4.
35. Fischer, op. cit., p. 263.
36. M. K. Gandhi, 'How to Serve the Cow' (Ahmedabad).
37. John Grigg, 'A Quest for Gandhi', *Sunday Times*, 28 September 1969.
38. In *Harijan*, 17 February 1938.
39. Ashe, op. cit., p. 341.
40. Raman, op. cit., p. 24.
41. In Louis Fischer, ed., *The Essential Gandhi: An Anthology* (London, 1963). p. 334.
42. ibid., p. 125.
43. Louis Fischer, op. cit., p. 371.
44. In Fischer, *The Essential Gandhi*, p. 125.
45. Bose, op. cit., pp. 104, 107.
46. ibid., pp. 149–50.
47. ibid., pp. 244–5.
48. ibid., p. 251.
49. In *New Statesman*, 30 April 1949.
50. Bose, op. cit., p. 4n.
51. ibid., pp. 270–71.
52. ibid., p. 289.
53. Pyarelal, op. cit., Vol. II, pp. 685–6.
54. In Chandrashanker Shukla, ed., *Incidents of Ghandhiji's Life* (Bombay, 1949), p. 85.

55. In *Talking of Gandhiji : Four Programmes for Radio* first broadcast by the British Broadcasting Corporation, script and narration by Francis Watson, production by Maurice Brown (London, New York and Toronto, 1957), p. 14.
56. Raman, op. cit., p. 88.

B₁